MYTHOLOGY GRAPHICS

THE TROJAN HORSE

A MODERN GRAPHIC GREEK MYTH

BY STEPHANIE PETERS
ILLUSTRATED BY OSCAR HERRERO
COVER BY LE NHAT VU

CAPSTONE PRESS
a capstone imprint

Published by Capstone Press, an imprint of Capstone
1710 Roe Crest Drive, North Mankato, Minnesota 56003
www.capstonepub.com

Library of Congress Cataloging-in-Publication Data is available
on the Library of Congress website.

ISBN: 9781669051015 (hardcover)
ISBN: 9781669050964 (paperback)
ISBN: 9781669050971 (ebook PDF)

Summary: The Greek goddesses can be competitive—especially when it comes to
being "the fairest." When Aphrodite, the goddess of love, wins the title, it kicks off
a ten-year battle between the Greeks and the Trojans. Find out who comes out on
top—and how the Trojan horse came to be—in this modern, graphic retelling of
a classic Greek myth.

Editorial Credits:
Editor: Alison Deering; Designer: Jaime Willems;
Production Specialist: Whitney Schaefer

All internet sites appearing in back matter were available and accurate
when this book was sent to press.

Printed and bound in the USA. PO#5425

TABLE OF CONTENTS

Chapter 1
Oh, I'm Judging You 4

Chapter 2
Anybody Know Where Troy Is? 12

Chapter 3
Hurry Up and Wait 18

Chapter 4
Year Ten: Attack! 26

Chapter 5
Try a Little Cleverness 34

More About the Trojan Horse 44

Glossary 46

Internet Sites 47

Other Books in This Series 47

About the Creators 48

CHAPTER 1

OH, I'M JUDGING YOU

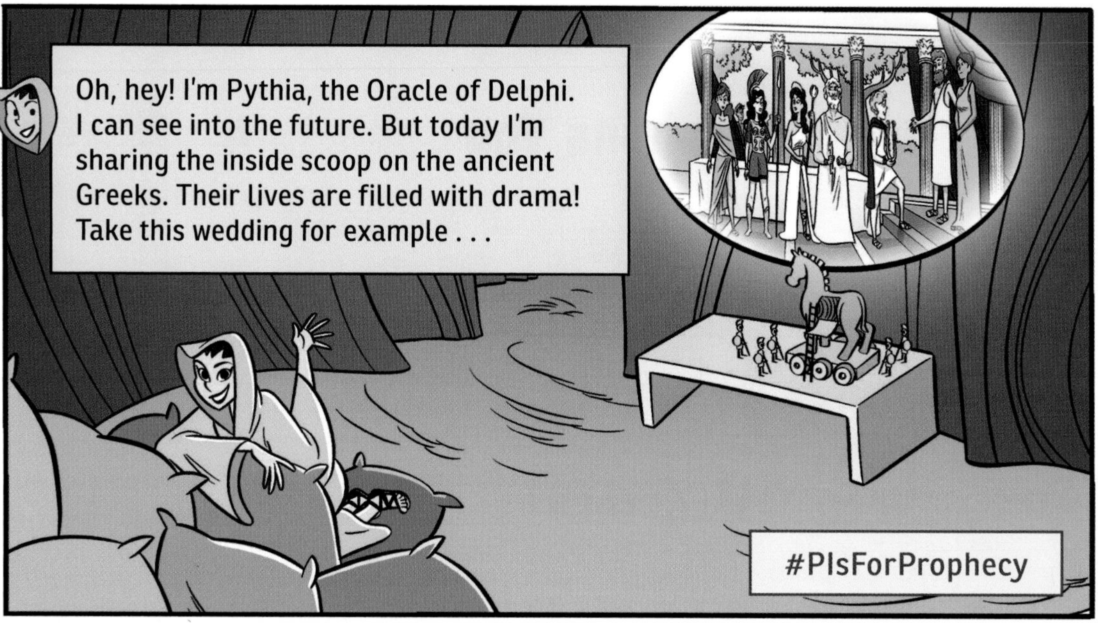
Oh, hey! I'm Pythia, the Oracle of Delphi. I can see into the future. But today I'm sharing the inside scoop on the ancient Greeks. Their lives are filled with drama! Take this wedding for example . . .
#PIsForProphecy

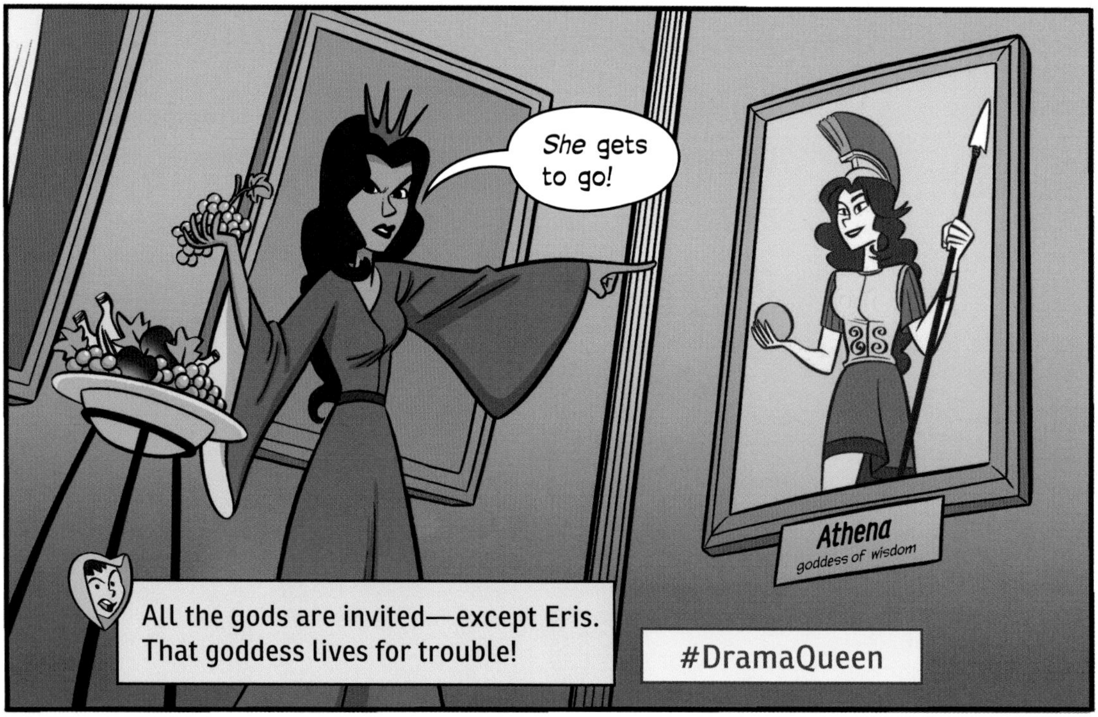
She gets to go!
Athena
goddess of wisdom
All the gods are invited—except Eris. That goddess lives for trouble!
#DramaQueen

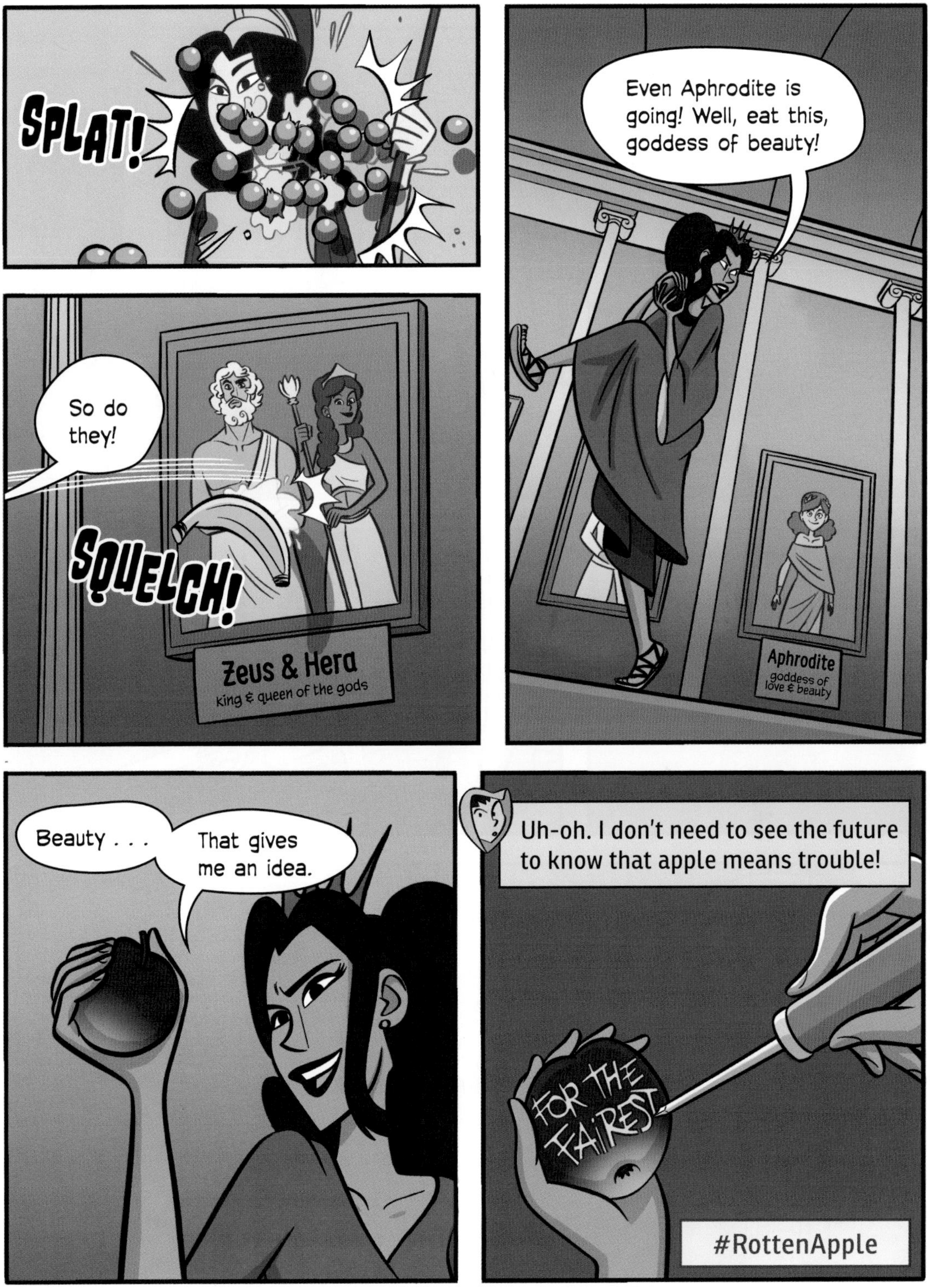
SPLAT!
Even Aphrodite is going! Well, eat this, goddess of beauty!
So do they!
SQUELCH!
Zeus & Hera
King & queen of the gods
Aphrodite
goddess of love & beauty
Beauty . . .
That gives me an idea.
Uh-oh. I don't need to see the future to know that apple means trouble!
FOR THE FAIREST
#RottenApple

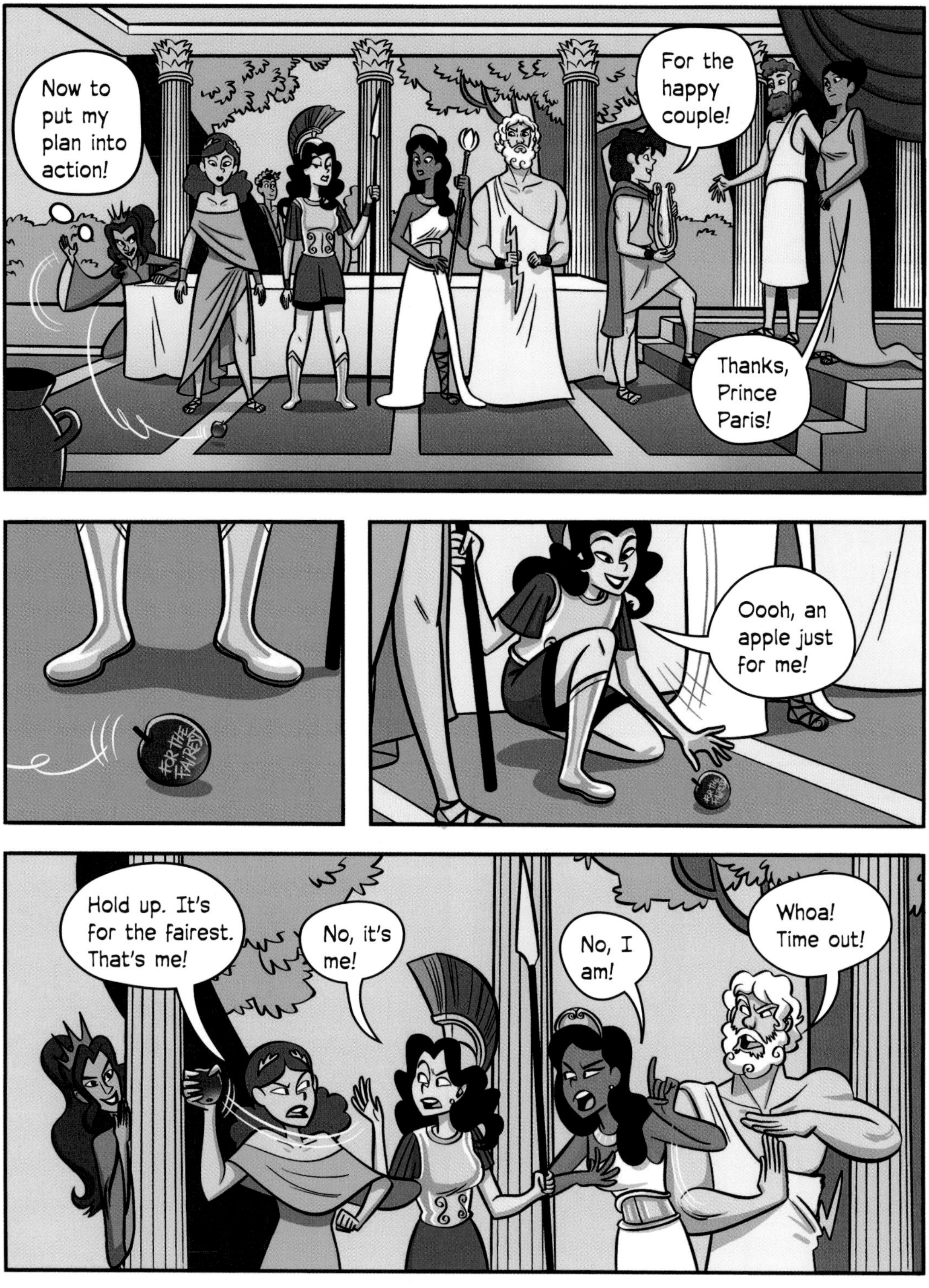
Now to put my plan into action!
For the happy couple!
Thanks, Prince Paris!
FOR THE FAIREST
Oooh, an apple just for me!
Hold up. It's for the fairest. That's me!
No, it's me!
No, I am!
Whoa! Time out!

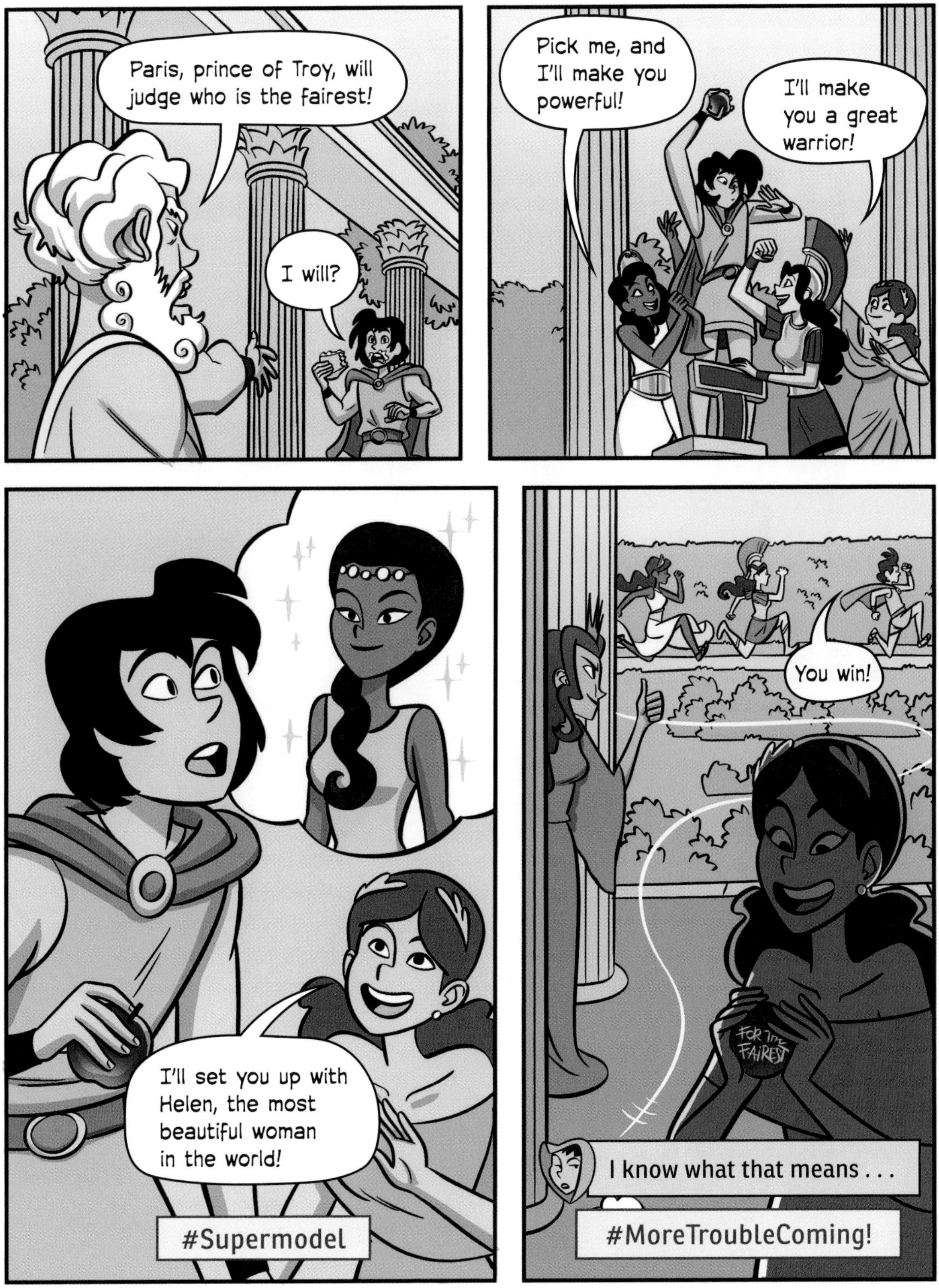
Paris, prince of Troy, will judge who is the fairest!
I will?
Pick me, and I'll make you powerful!
I'll make you a great warrior!
I'll set you up with Helen, the most beautiful woman in the world!
#Supermodel
You win!
FOR THE FAIREST
I know what that means . . .
#MoreTroubleComing!

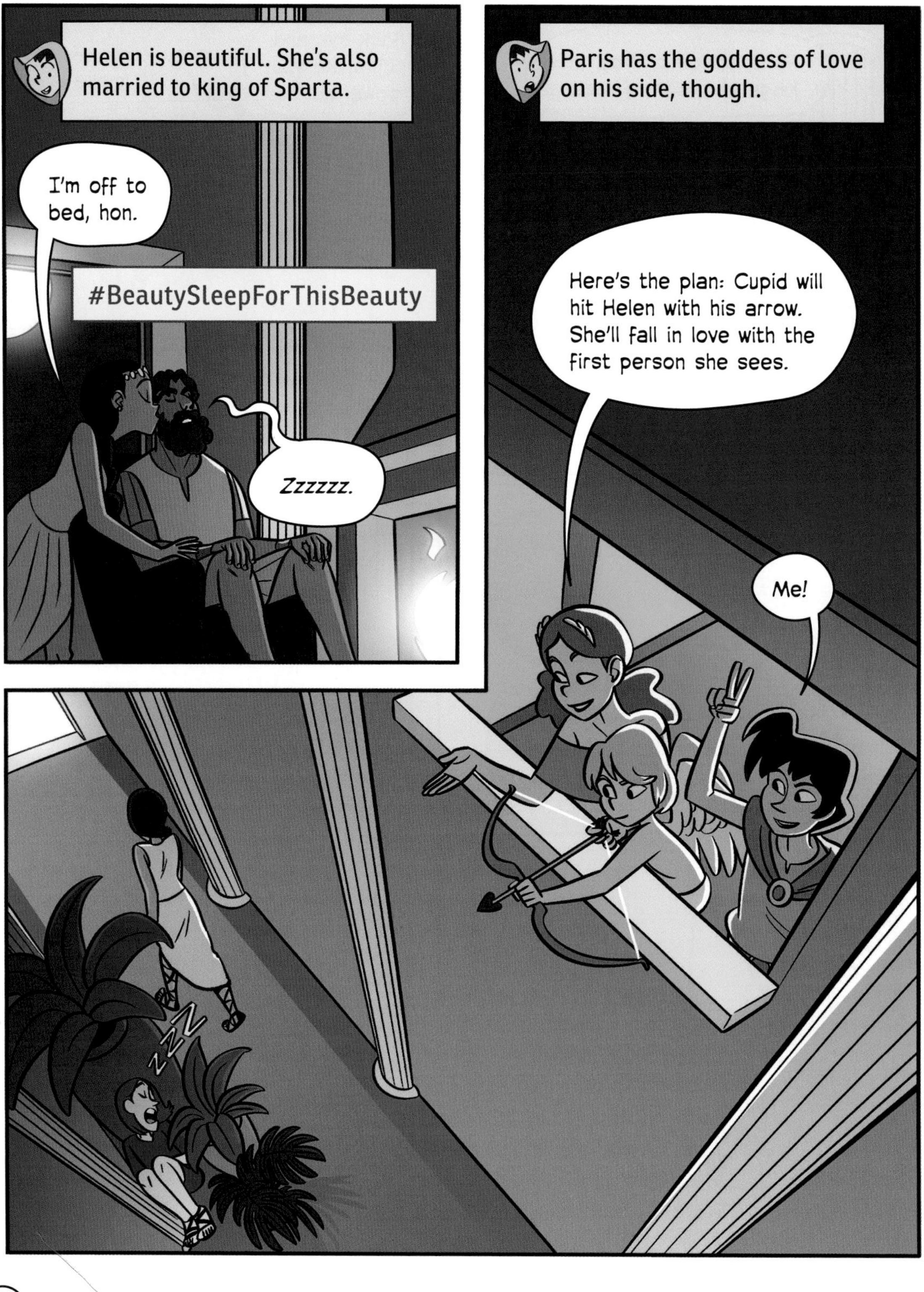
Helen is beautiful. She's also married to king of Sparta.
I'm off to bed, hon.
#BeautySleepForThisBeauty
Zzzzzz.
Paris has the goddess of love on his side, though.
Here's the plan: Cupid will hit Helen with his arrow. She'll fall in love with the first person she sees.
Me!
Z
Z
Z

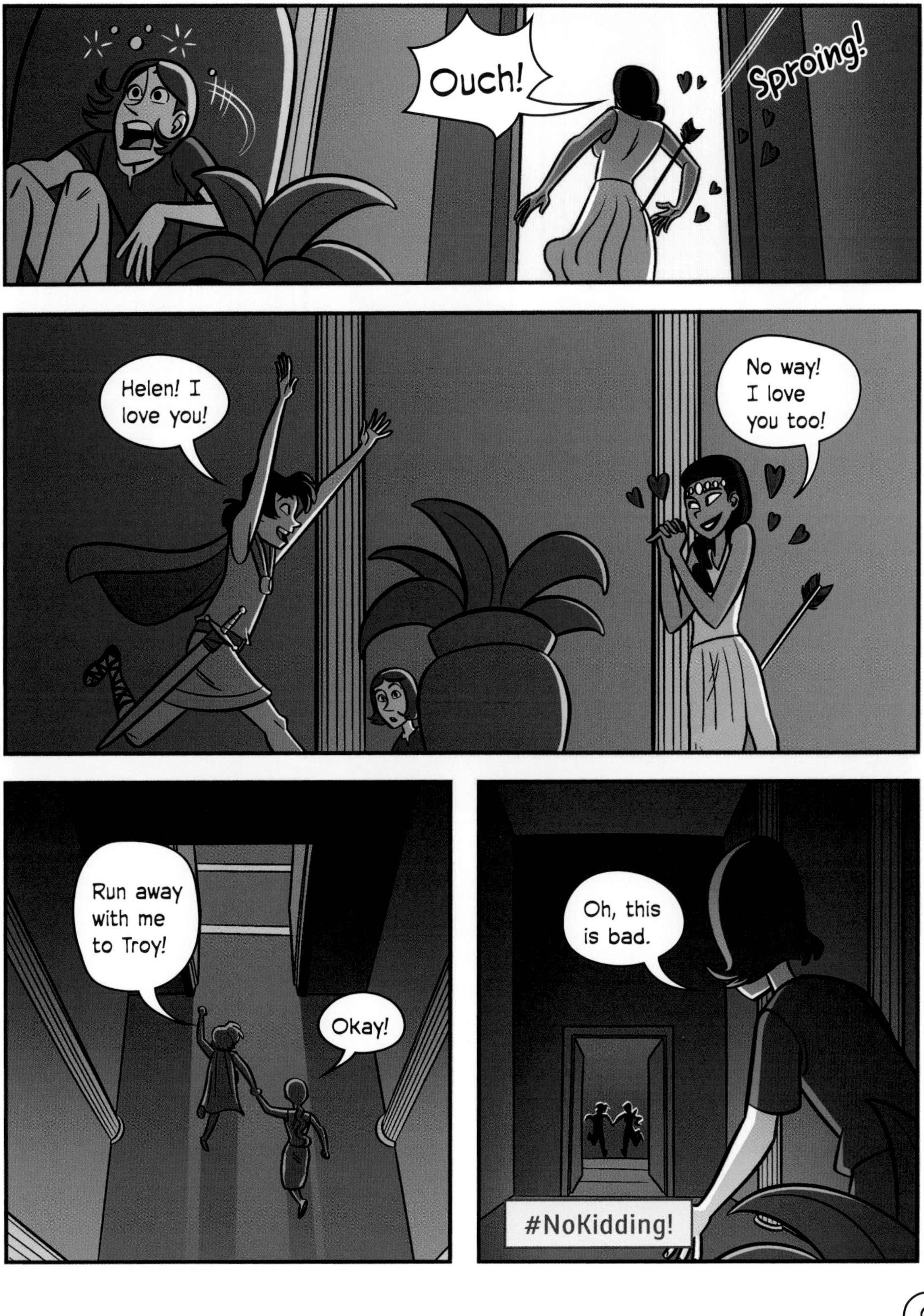
Ouch!
Sproing!
Helen! I love you!
No way! I love you too!
Run away with me to Troy!
Okay!
Oh, this is bad.
#NoKidding!

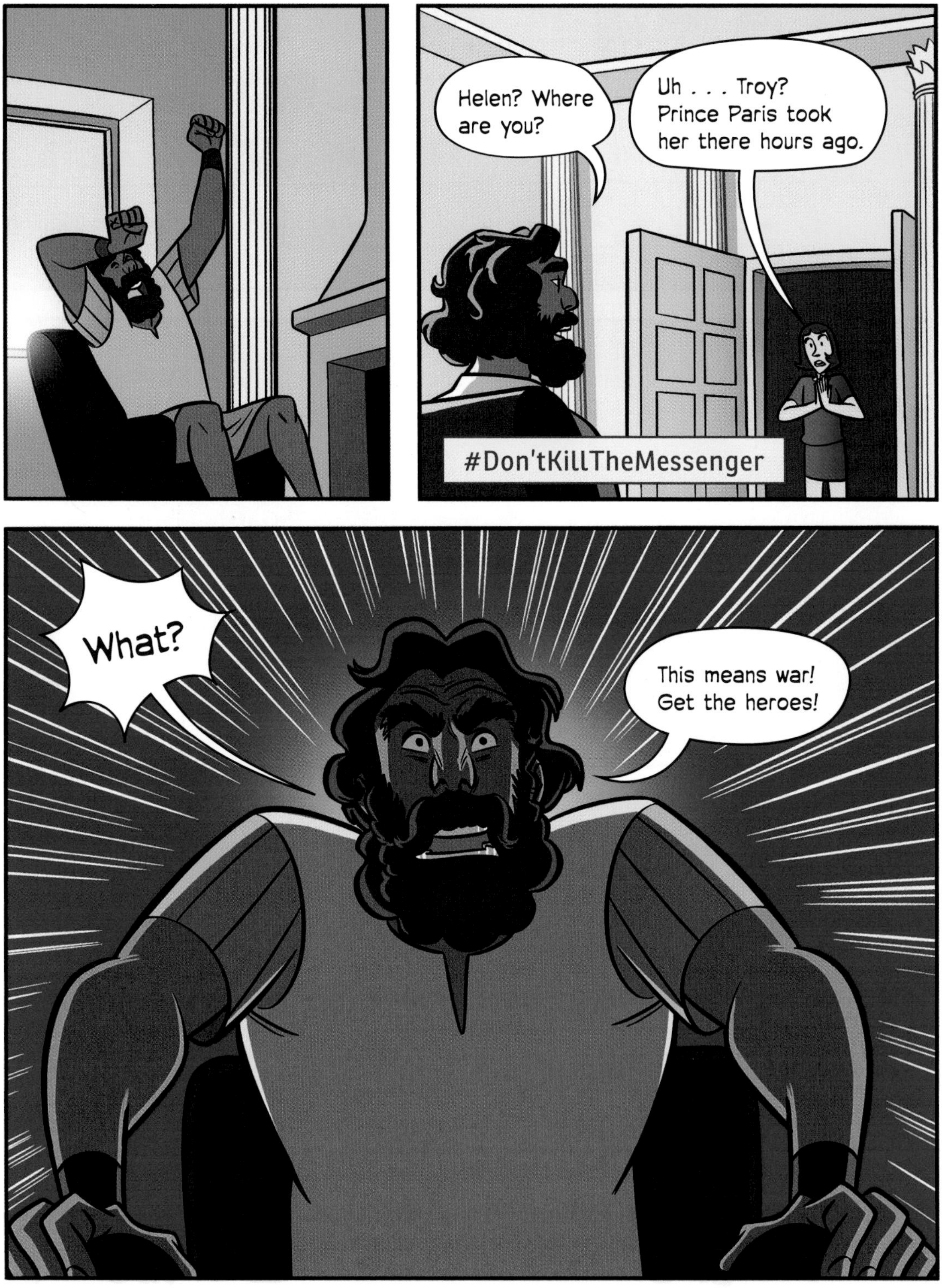
Helen? Where are you?
Uh . . . Troy? Prince Paris took her there hours ago.
#Don'tKillTheMessenger
What?
This means war! Get the heroes!

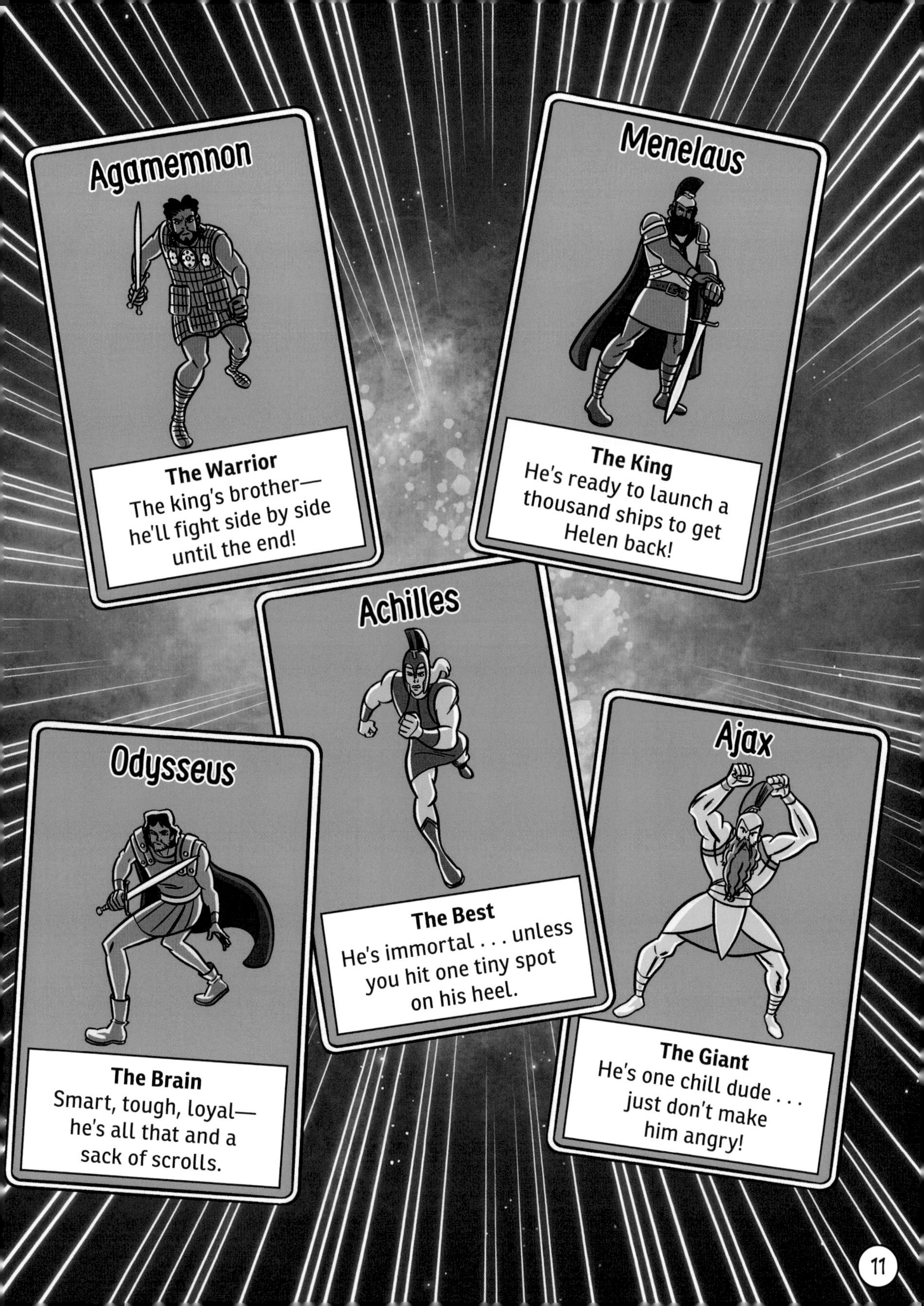

Agamemnon
The Warrior
The king's brother—he'll fight side by side until the end!
Menelaus
The King
He's ready to launch a thousand ships to get Helen back!
Achilles
The Best
He's immortal . . . unless you hit one tiny spot on his heel.
Odysseus
The Brain
Smart, tough, loyal—he's all that and a sack of scrolls.
Ajax
The Giant
He's one chill dude . . . just don't make him angry!

CHAPTER 2

Anybody Know Where Troy Is?

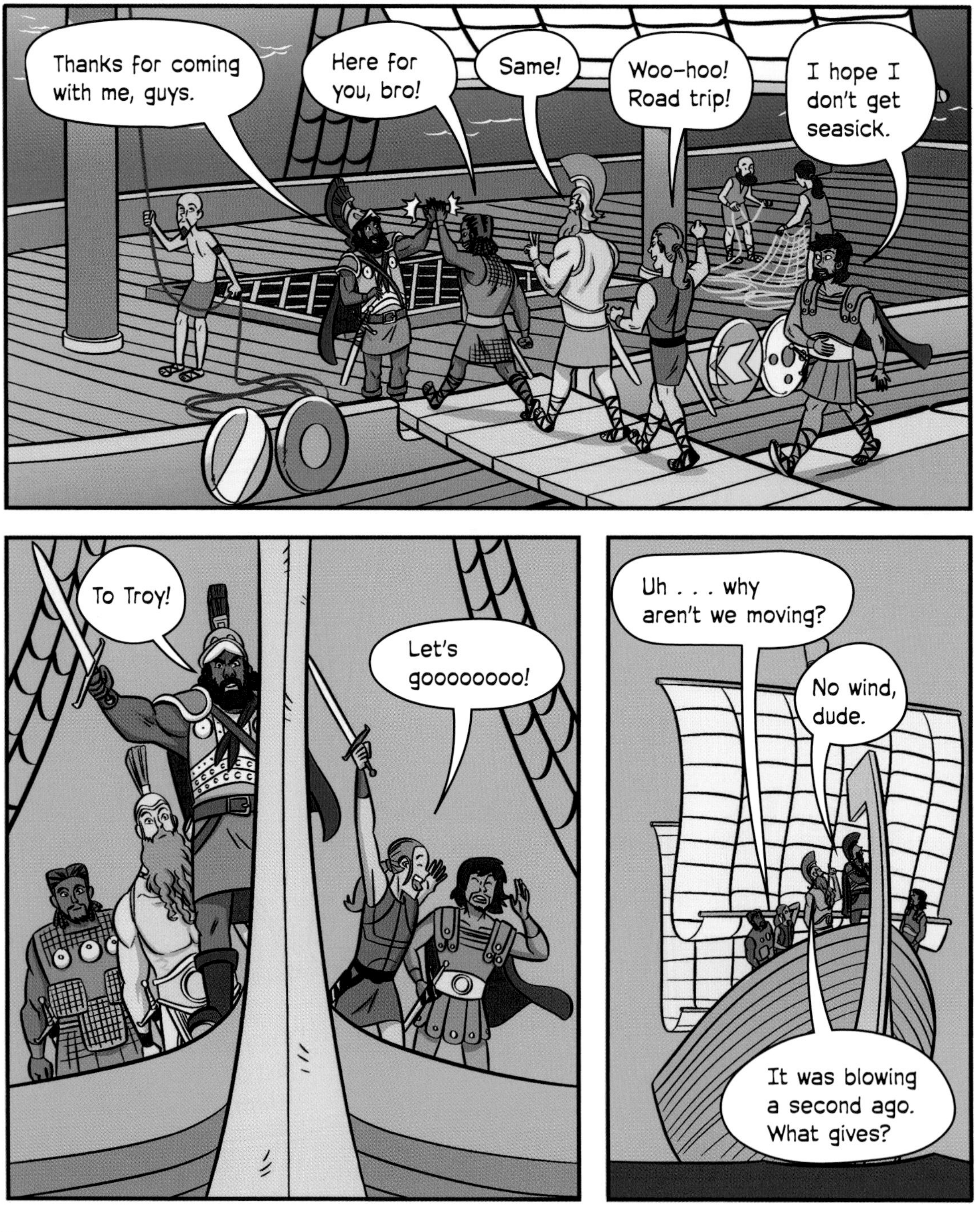
Thanks for coming with me, guys.
Here for you, bro!
Same!
Woo-hoo! Road trip!
I hope I don't get seasick.
To Troy!
Let's gooooooooo!
Uh . . . why aren't we moving?
No wind, dude.
It was blowing a second ago. What gives?

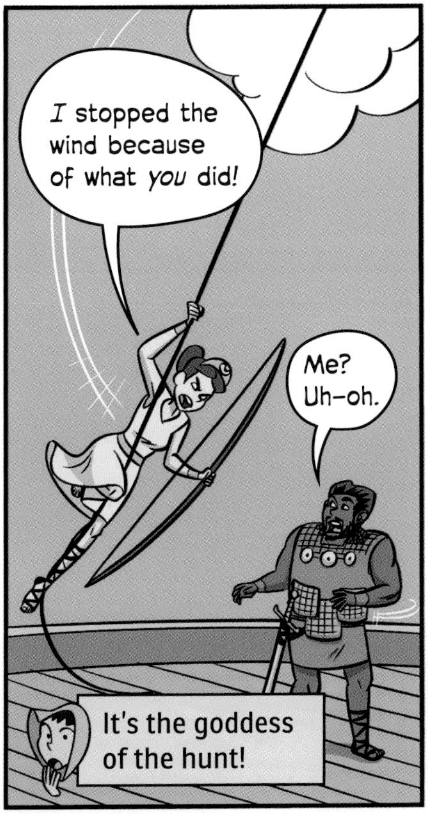
I stopped the wind because of what you did!
Me? Uh-oh.
It's the goddess of the hunt!

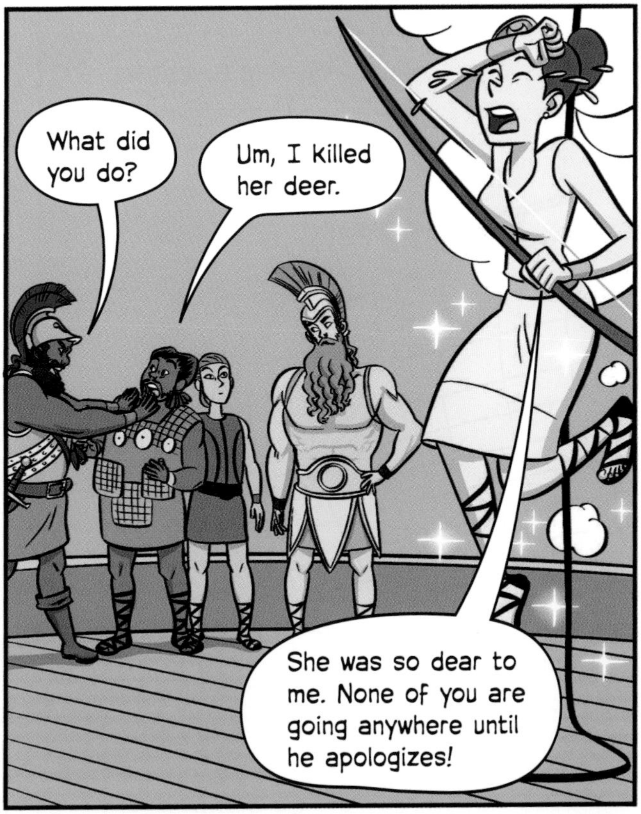
What did you do?
Um, I killed her deer.
She was so dear to me. None of you are going anywhere until he apologizes!

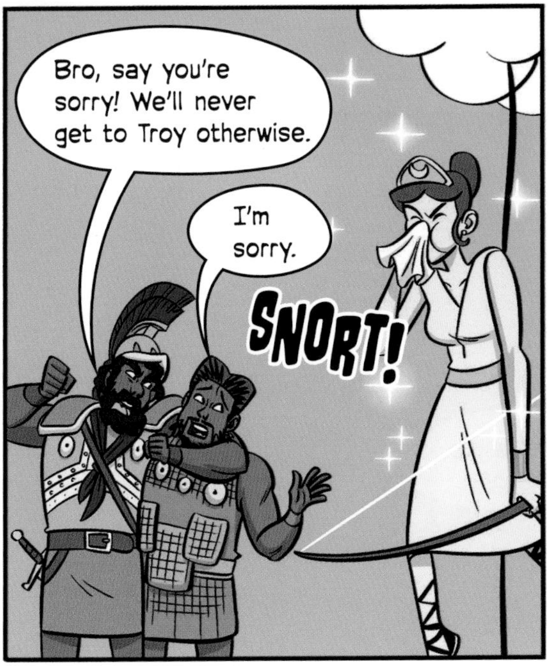
Bro, say you're sorry! We'll never get to Troy otherwise.
I'm sorry.
SNORT!

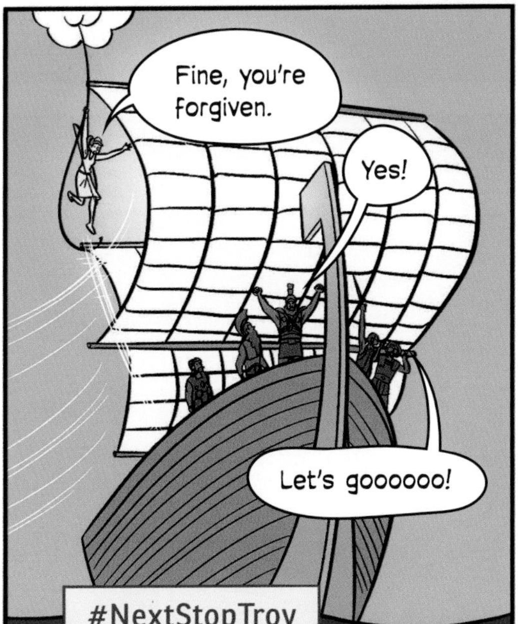
Fine, you're forgiven.
Yes!
Let's goooooo!
#NextStopTroy

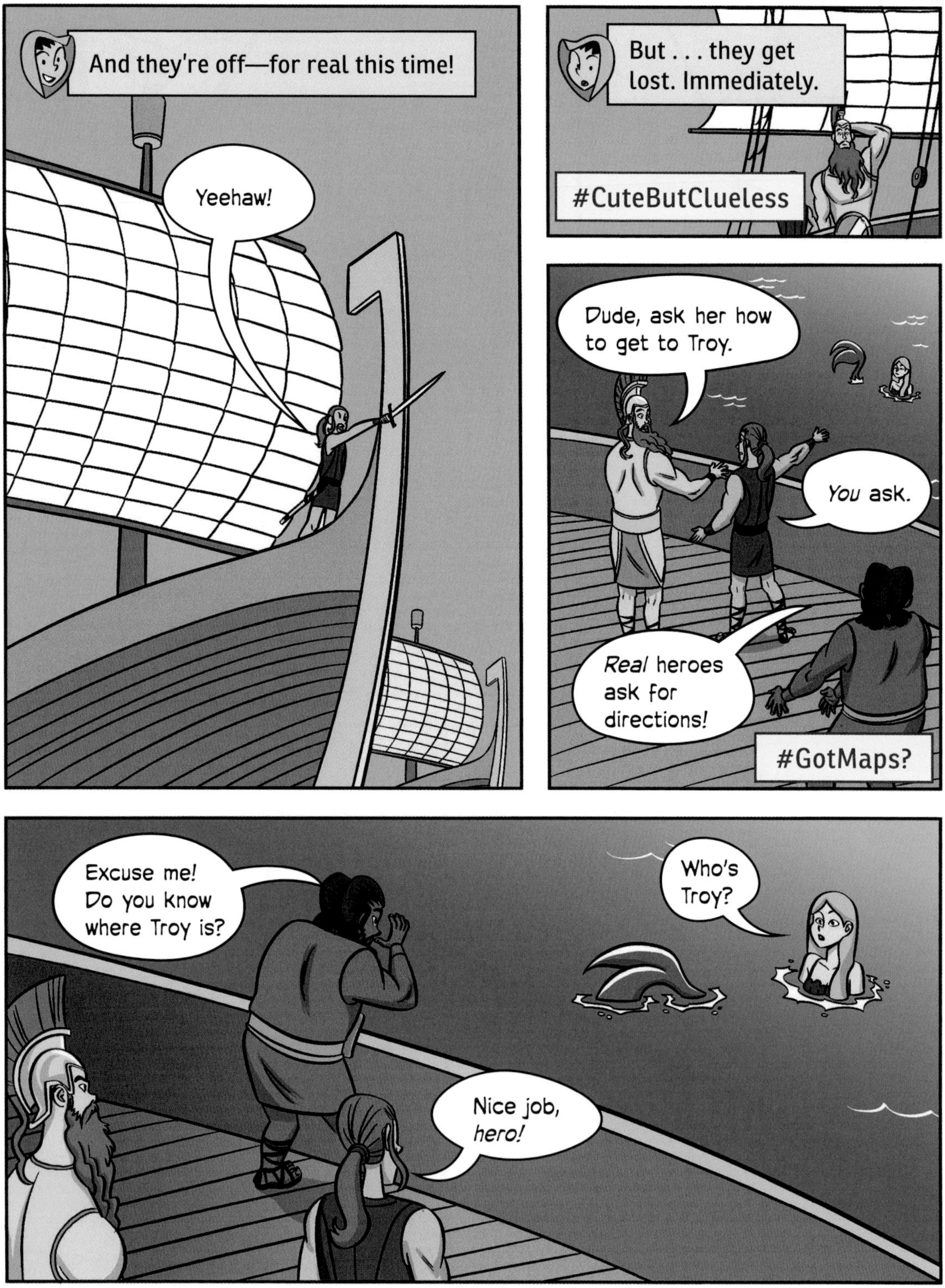
And they're off—for real this time!
Yeehaw!
But . . . they get lost. Immediately.
#CuteButClueless
Dude, ask her how to get to Troy.
You ask.
Real heroes ask for directions!
#GotMaps?
Excuse me! Do you know where Troy is?
Who's Troy?
Nice job, *hero!*

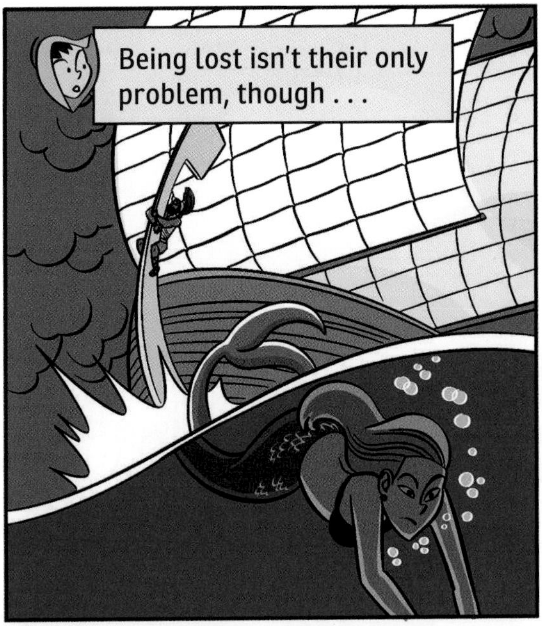
Being lost isn't their only problem, though . . .

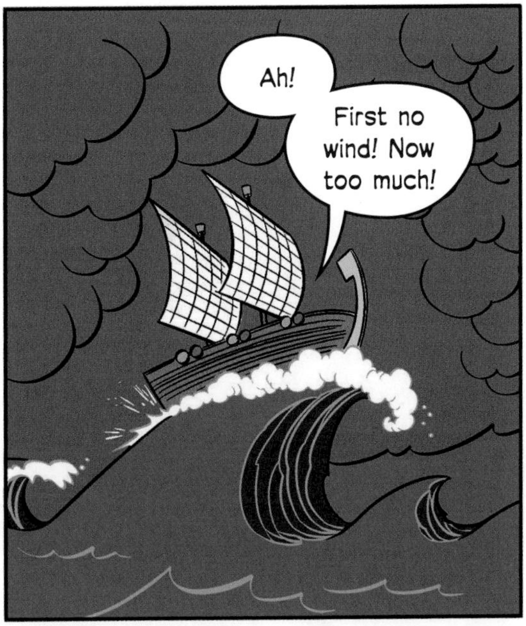
Ah!
First no wind! Now too much!

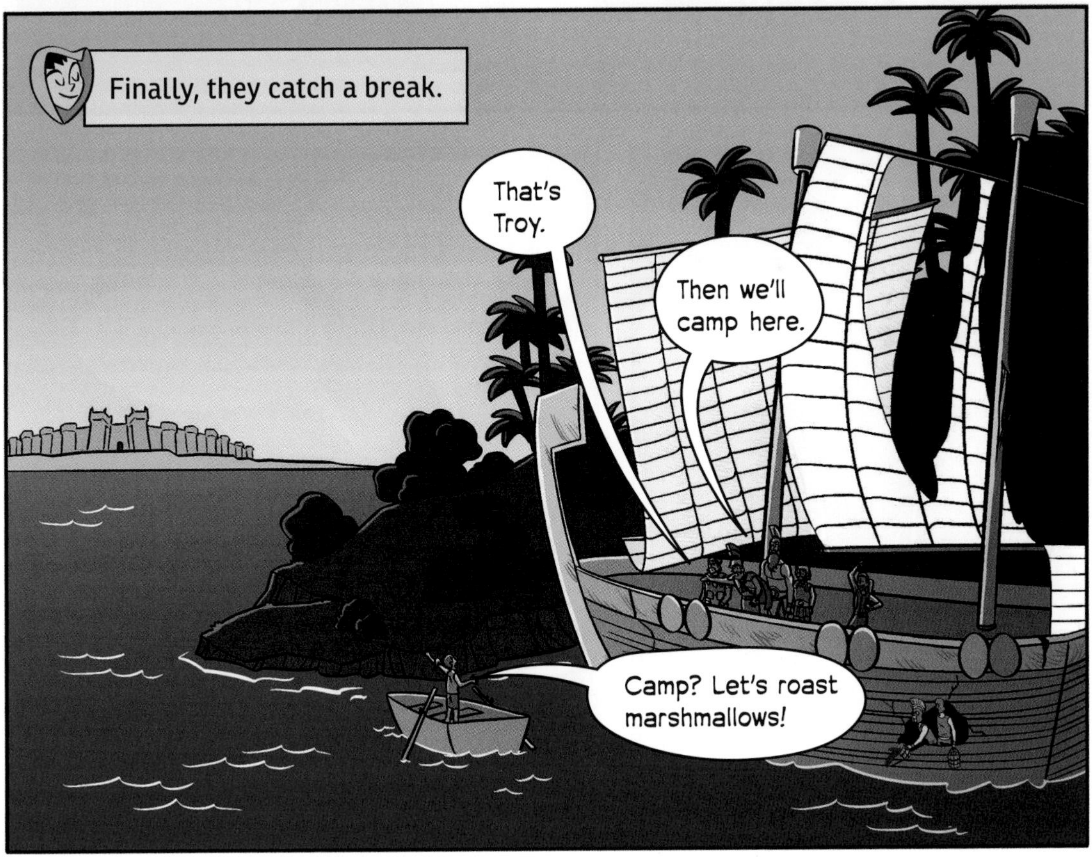
Finally, they catch a break.
That's Troy.
Then we'll camp here.
Camp? Let's roast marshmallows!

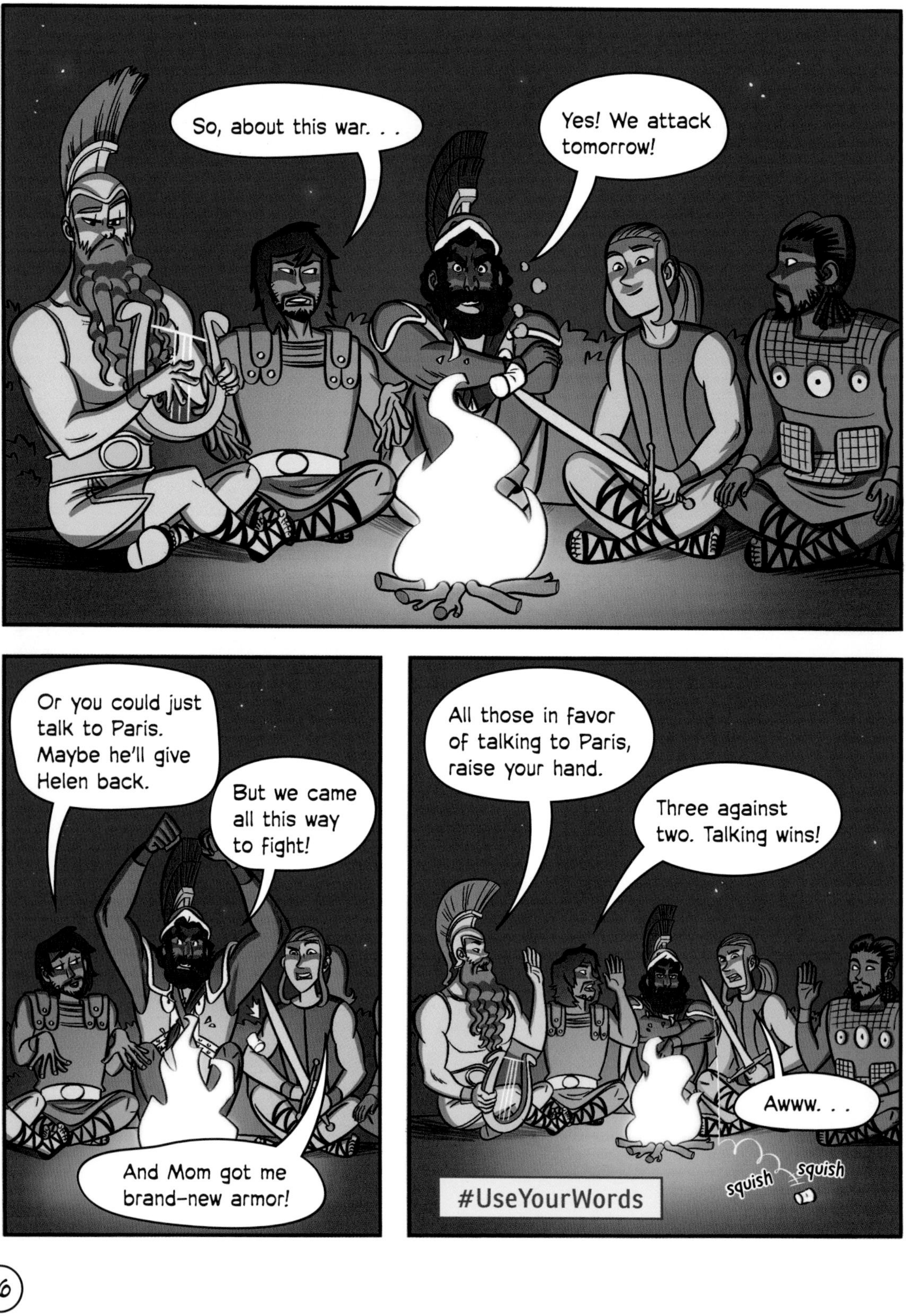
So, about this war. . .
Yes! We attack tomorrow!
Or you could just talk to Paris. Maybe he'll give Helen back.
But we came all this way to fight!
And Mom got me brand-new armor!
All those in favor of talking to Paris, raise your hand.
Three against two. Talking wins!
Awww. . .
squish
squish
#UseYourWords

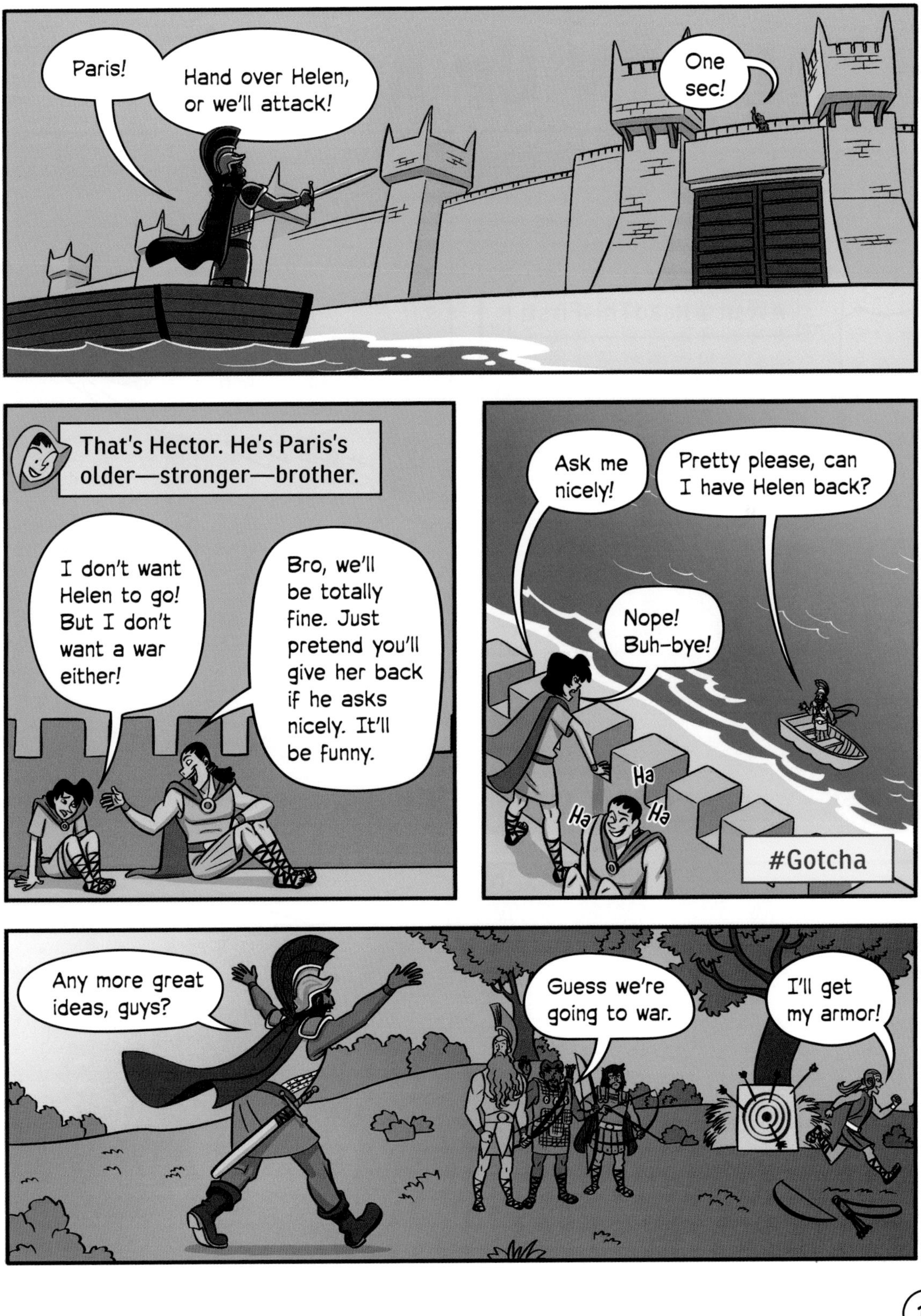
Paris!
Hand over Helen, or we'll attack!
One sec!
That's Hector. He's Paris's older—stronger—brother.
I don't want Helen to go! But I don't want a war either!
Bro, we'll be totally fine. Just pretend you'll give her back if he asks nicely. It'll be funny.
Ask me nicely!
Pretty please, can I have Helen back?
Nope! Buh-bye!
Ha
Ha
Ha
#Gotcha
Any more great ideas, guys?
Guess we're going to war.
I'll get my armor!

CHAPTER 3

HURRY UP AND WAIT

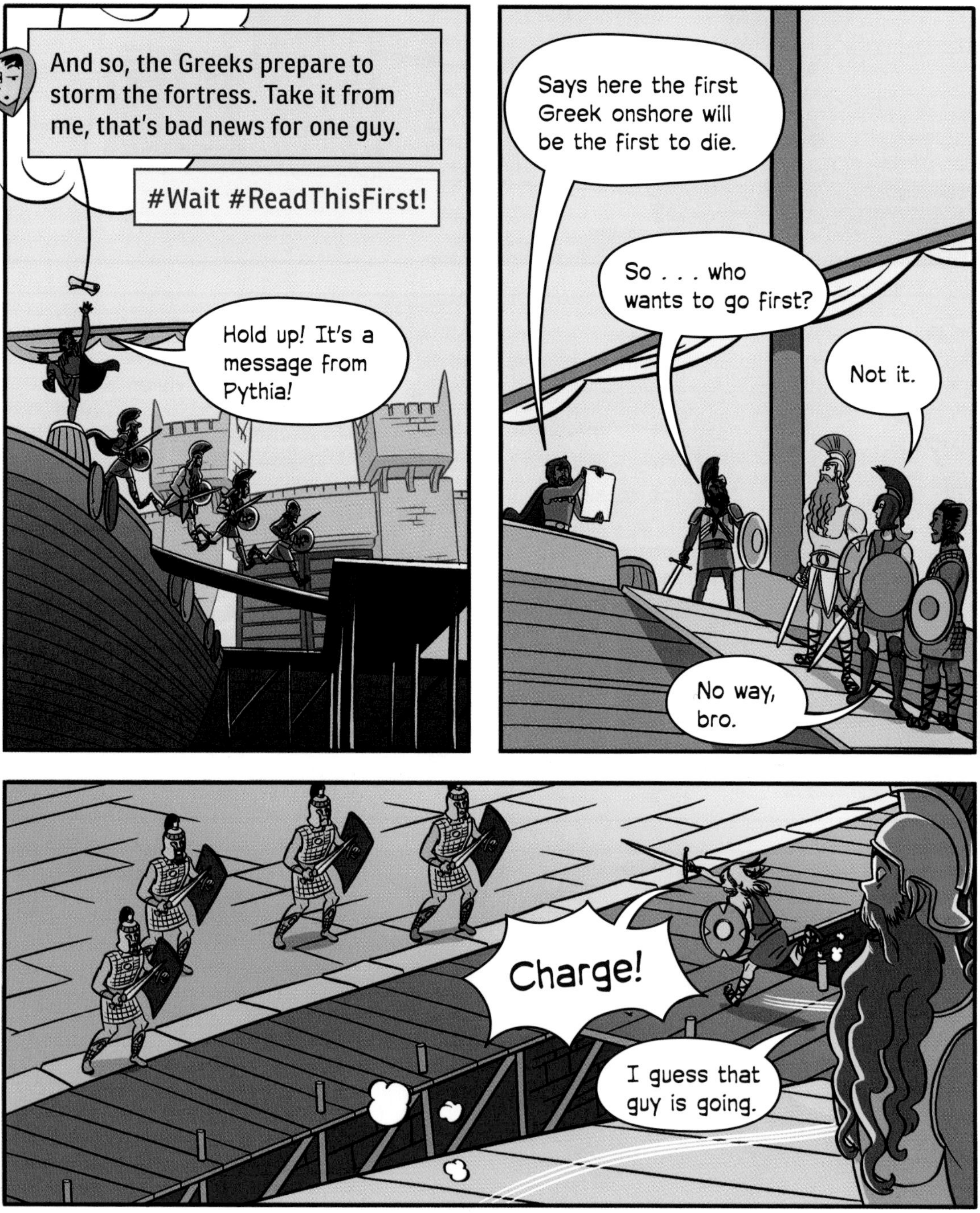
And so, the Greeks prepare to storm the fortress. Take it from me, that's bad news for one guy.
#Wait #ReadThisFirst!
Hold up! It's a message from Pythia!
Says here the first Greek onshore will be the first to die.
So . . . who wants to go first?
Not it.
No way, bro.
Charge!
I guess that guy is going.

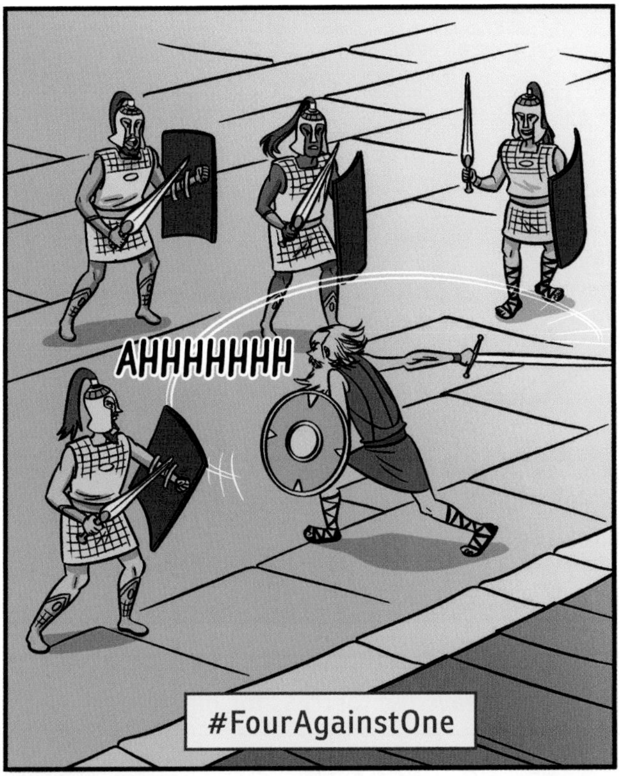
AHHHHHHH
#FourAgainstOne

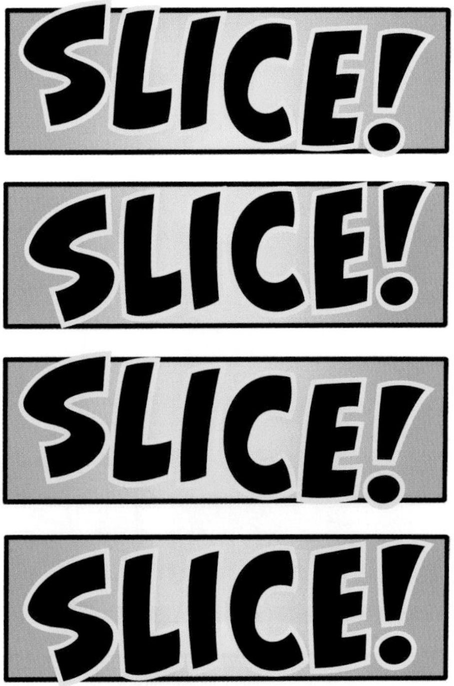
SLICE!
SLICE!
SLICE!
SLICE!

#OneBeatsFour

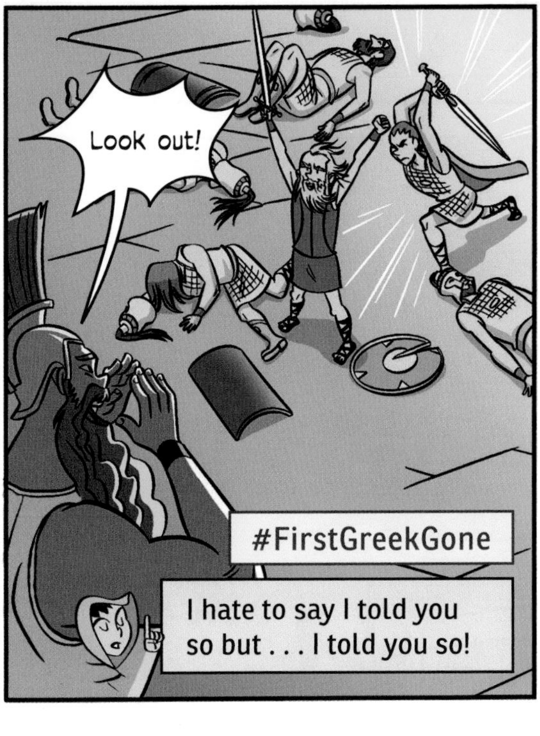
Look out!
#FirstGreekGone
I hate to say I told you so but . . . I told you so!

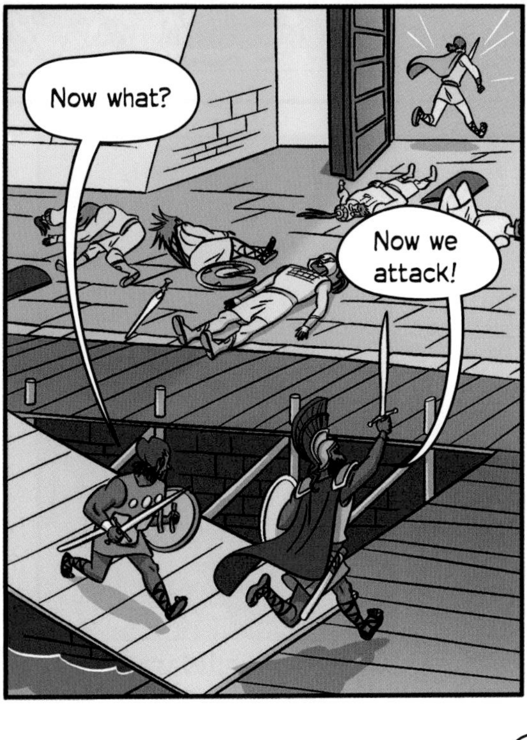
Now what?
Now we attack!

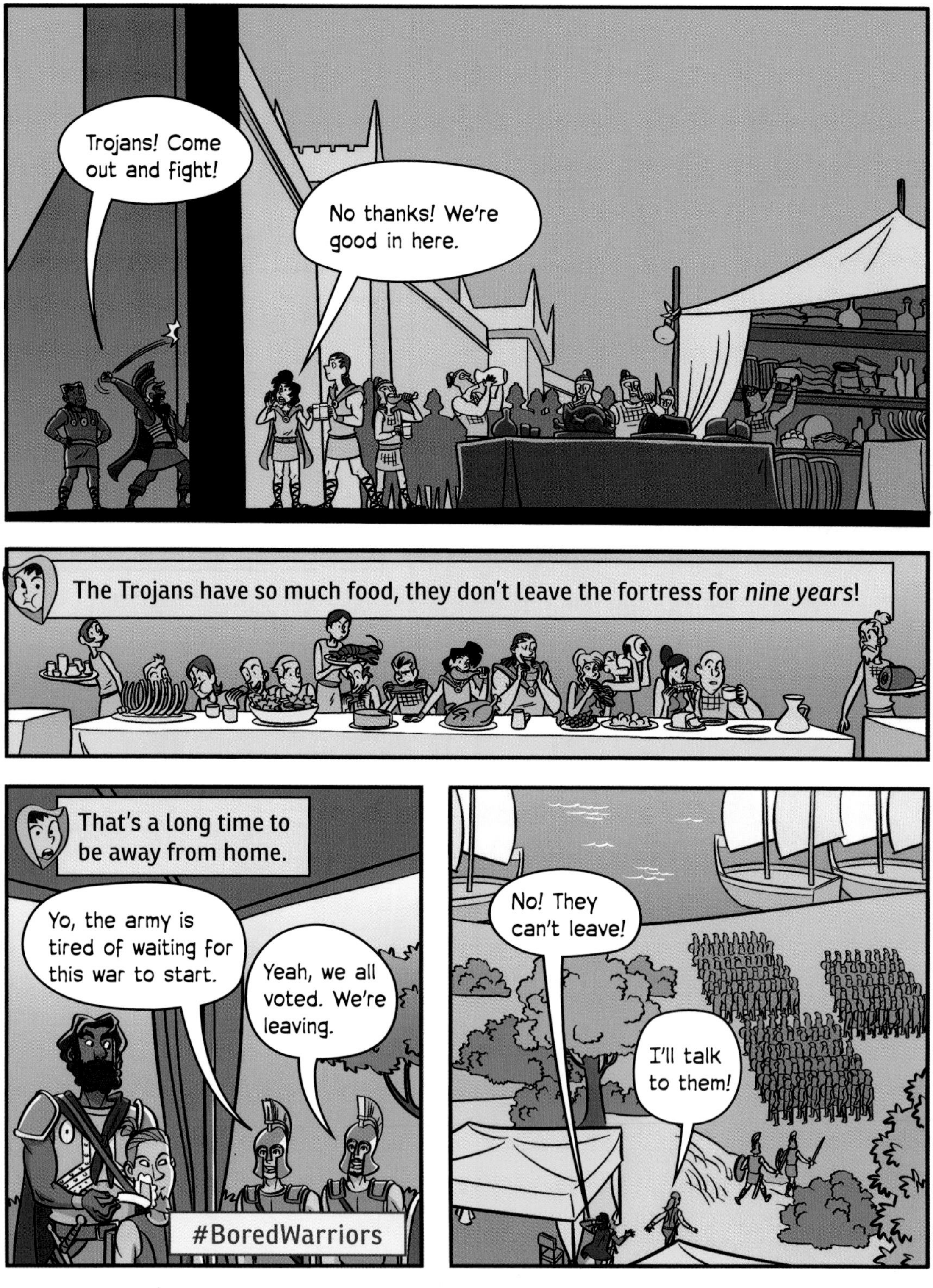
Trojans! Come out and fight!
No thanks! We're good in here.
The Trojans have so much food, they don't leave the fortress for *nine years*!
That's a long time to be away from home.
Yo, the army is tired of waiting for this war to start.
Yeah, we all voted. We're leaving.
#BoredWarriors
No! They can't leave!
I'll talk to them!

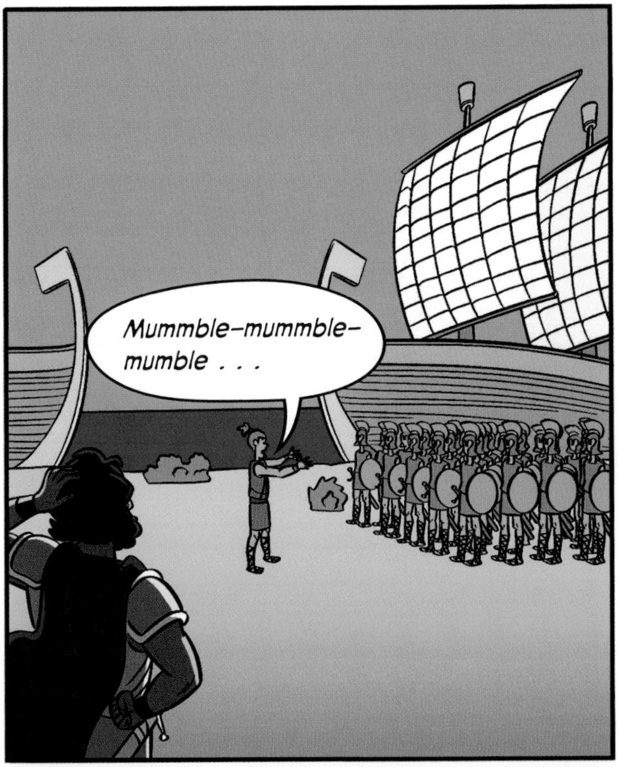
Mummble-mummble-mumble . . .

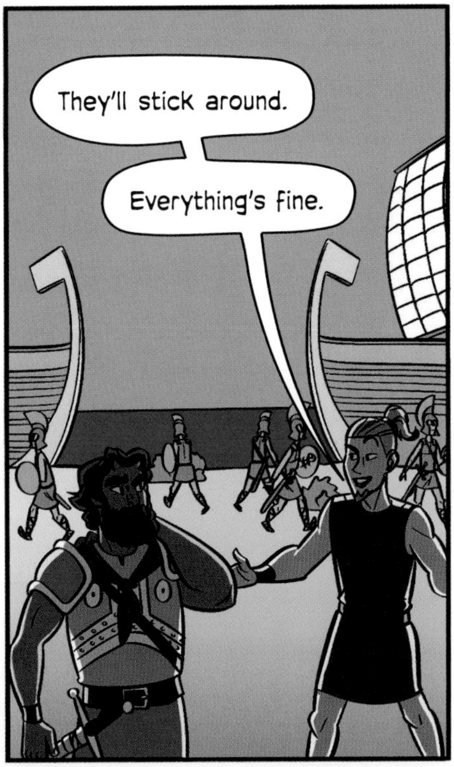
They'll stick around.
Everything's fine.

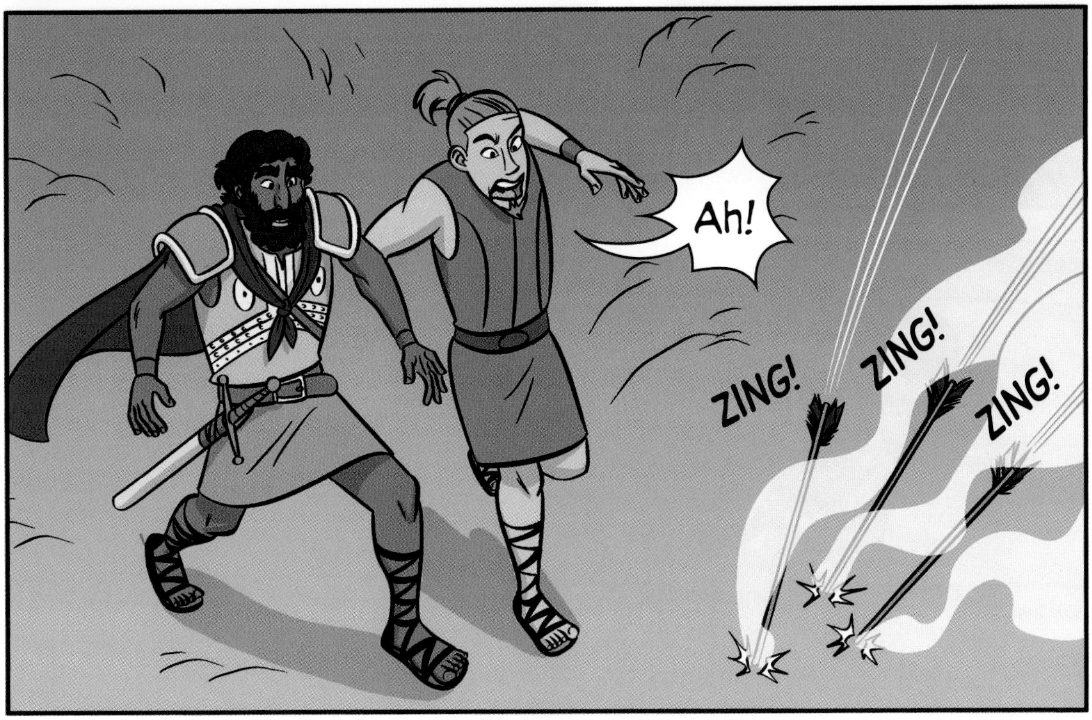
Ah!
ZING!
ZING!
ZING!

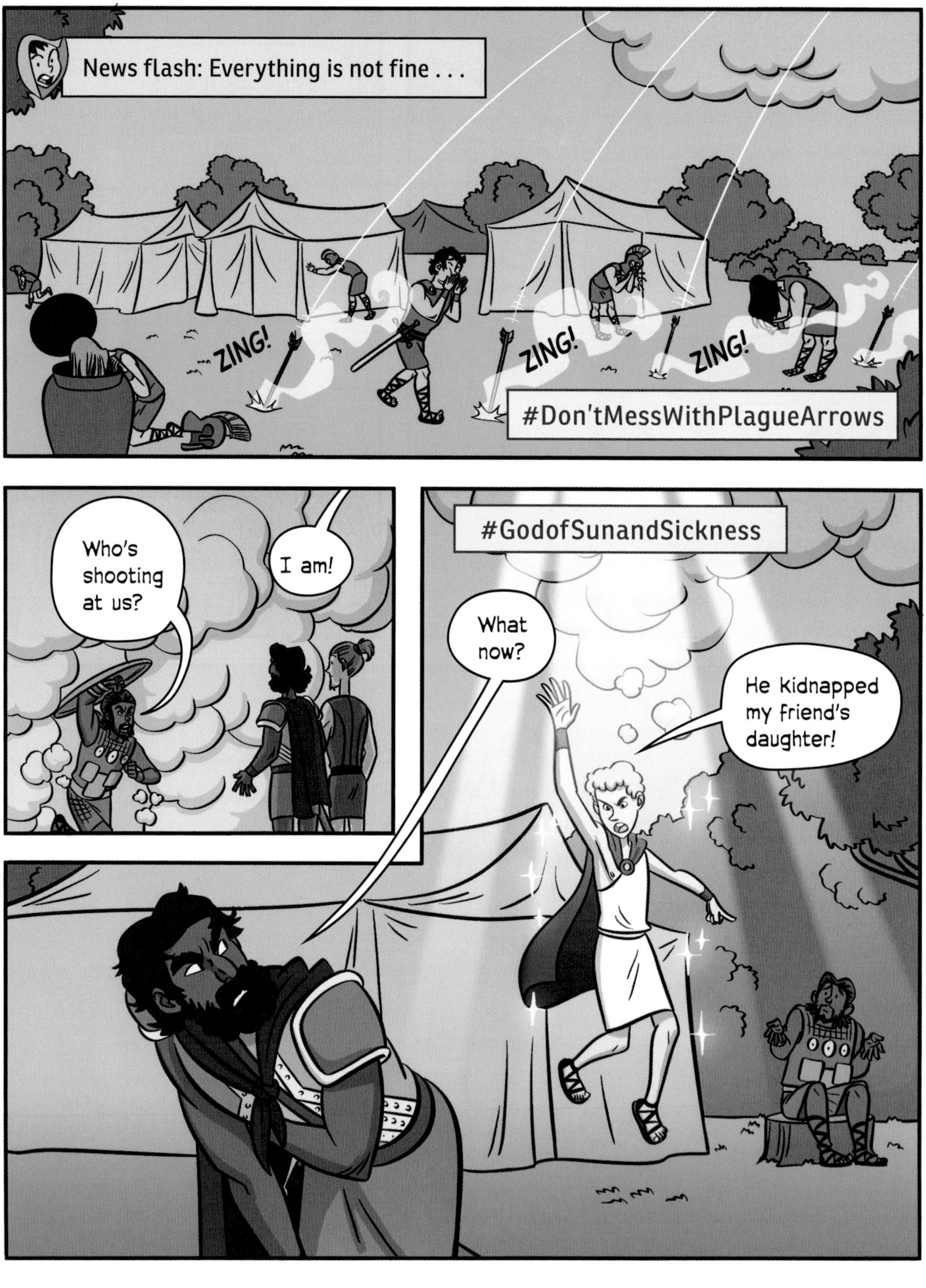
News flash: Everything is not fine . . .
ZING!
ZING!
ZING!
#Don'tMessWithPlagueArrows
Who's shooting at us?
I am!
#GodofSunandSickness
What now?
He kidnapped my friend's daughter!

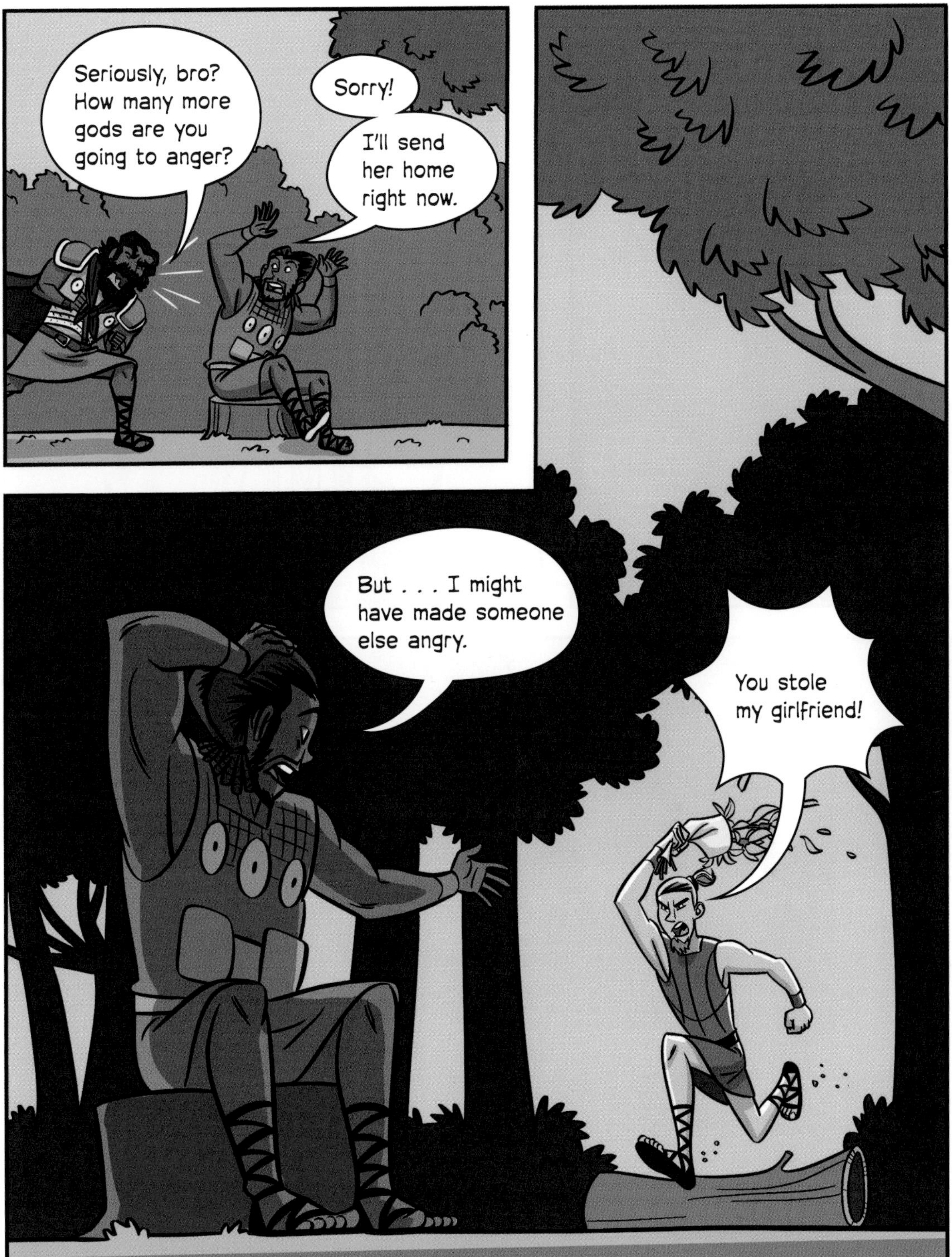
Seriously, bro? How many more gods are you going to anger?
Sorry!
I'll send her home right now.
But . . . I might have made someone else angry.
You stole my girlfriend!

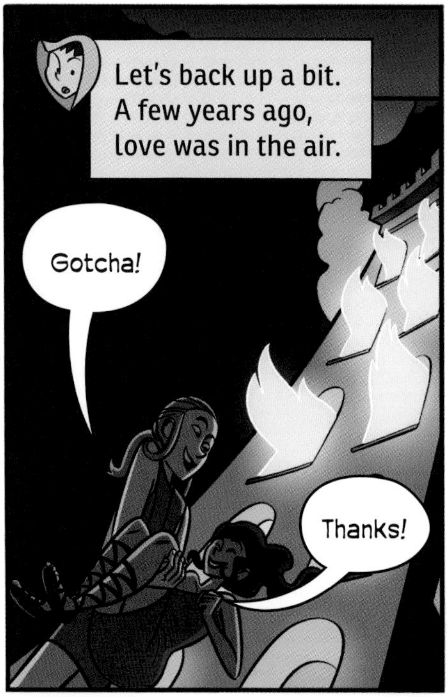
Let's back up a bit. A few years ago, love was in the air.
Gotcha!
Thanks!

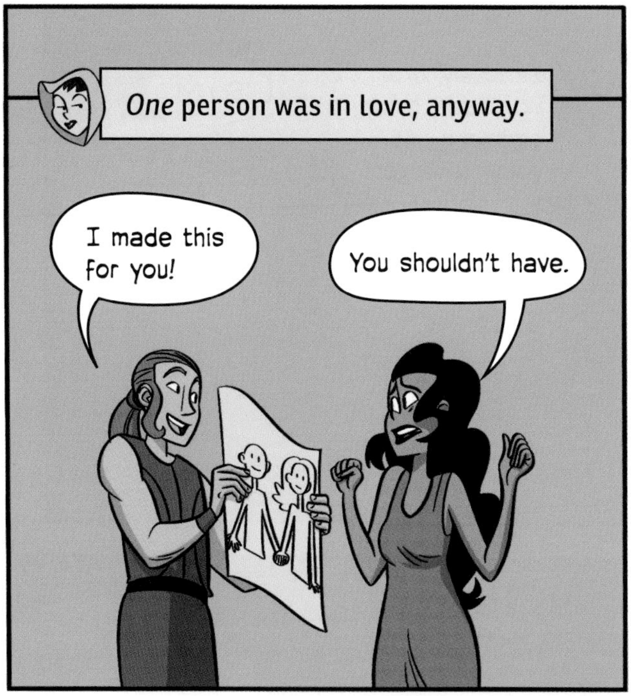
One person was in love, anyway.
I made this for you!
You shouldn't have.

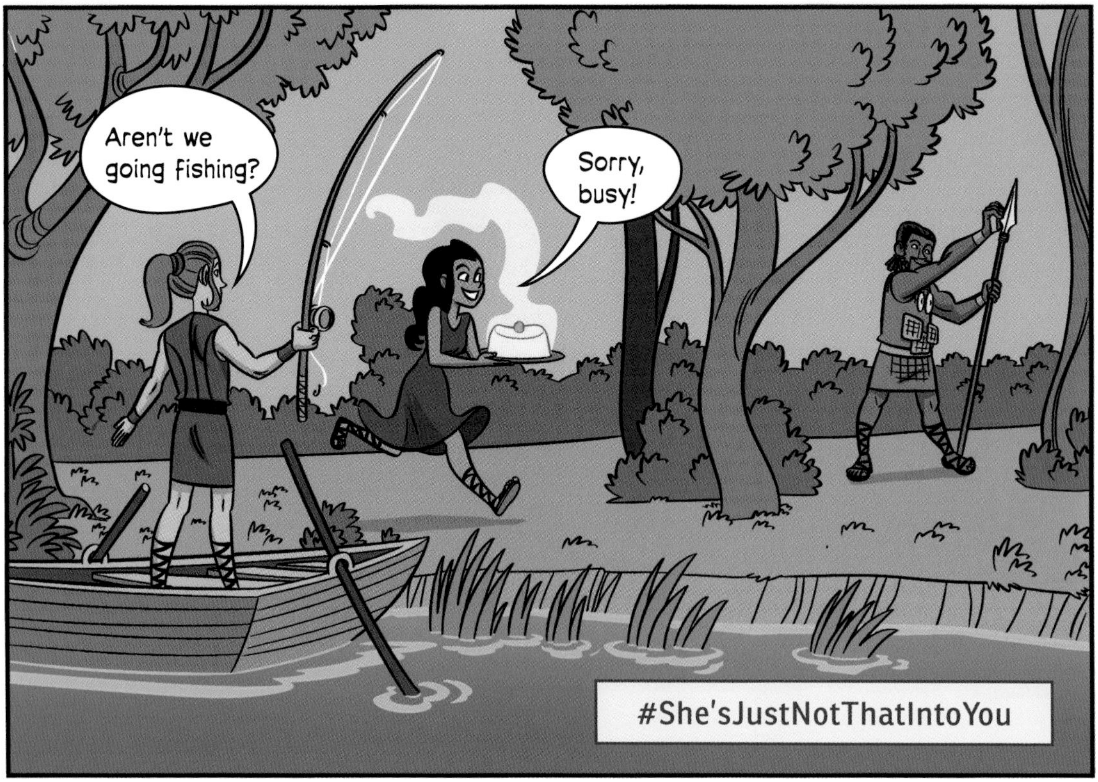
Aren't we going fishing?
Sorry, busy!
#She'sJustNotThatIntoYou

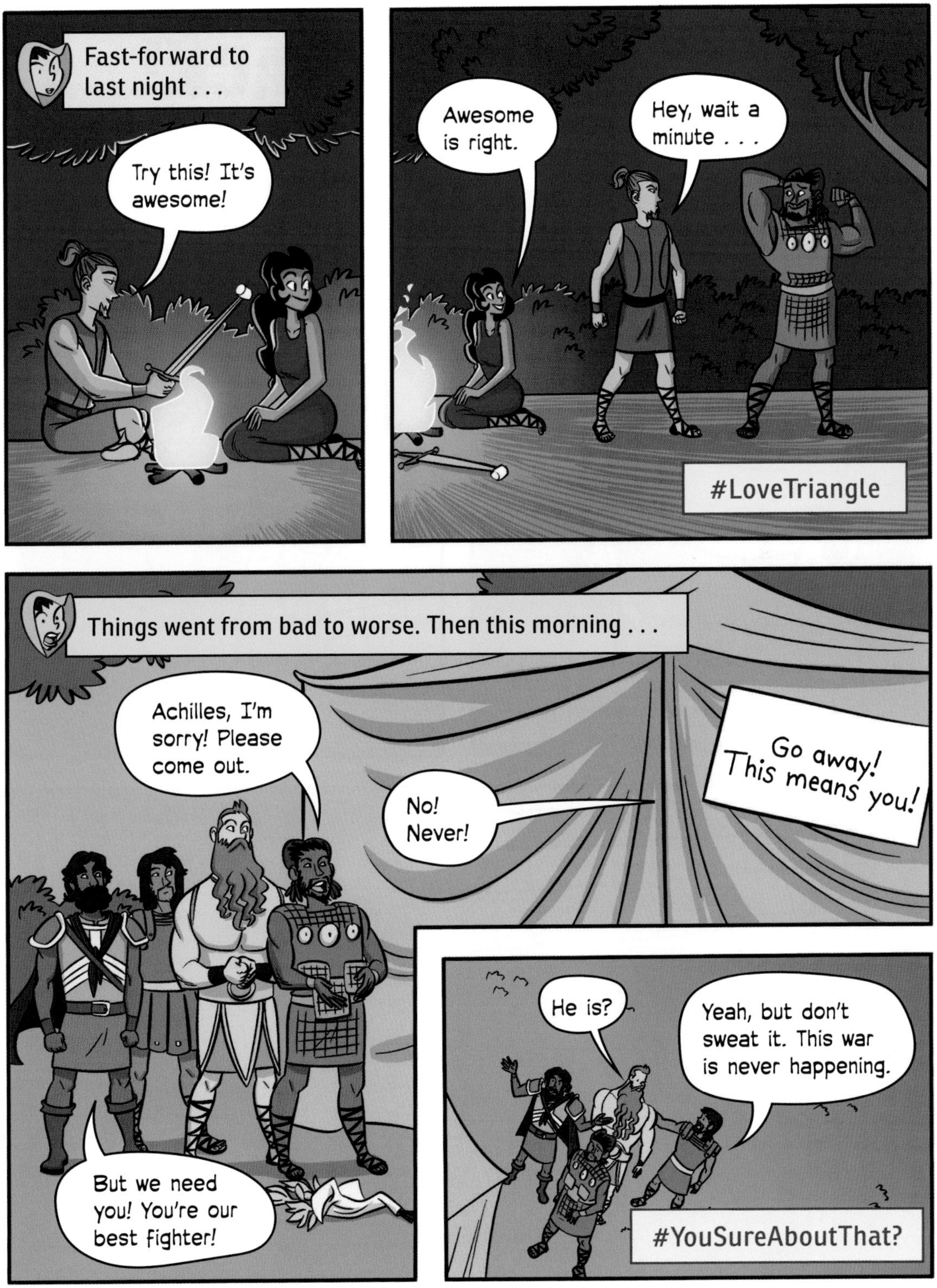

Fast-forward to last night . . .
Try this! It's awesome!
Awesome is right.
Hey, wait a minute . . .
#LoveTriangle
Things went from bad to worse. Then this morning . . .
Achilles, I'm sorry! Please come out.
No! Never!
Go away! This means you!
But we need you! You're our best fighter!
He is?
Yeah, but don't sweat it. This war is never happening.
#YouSureAboutThat?

CHAPTER 4

YEAR TEN: ATTACK!

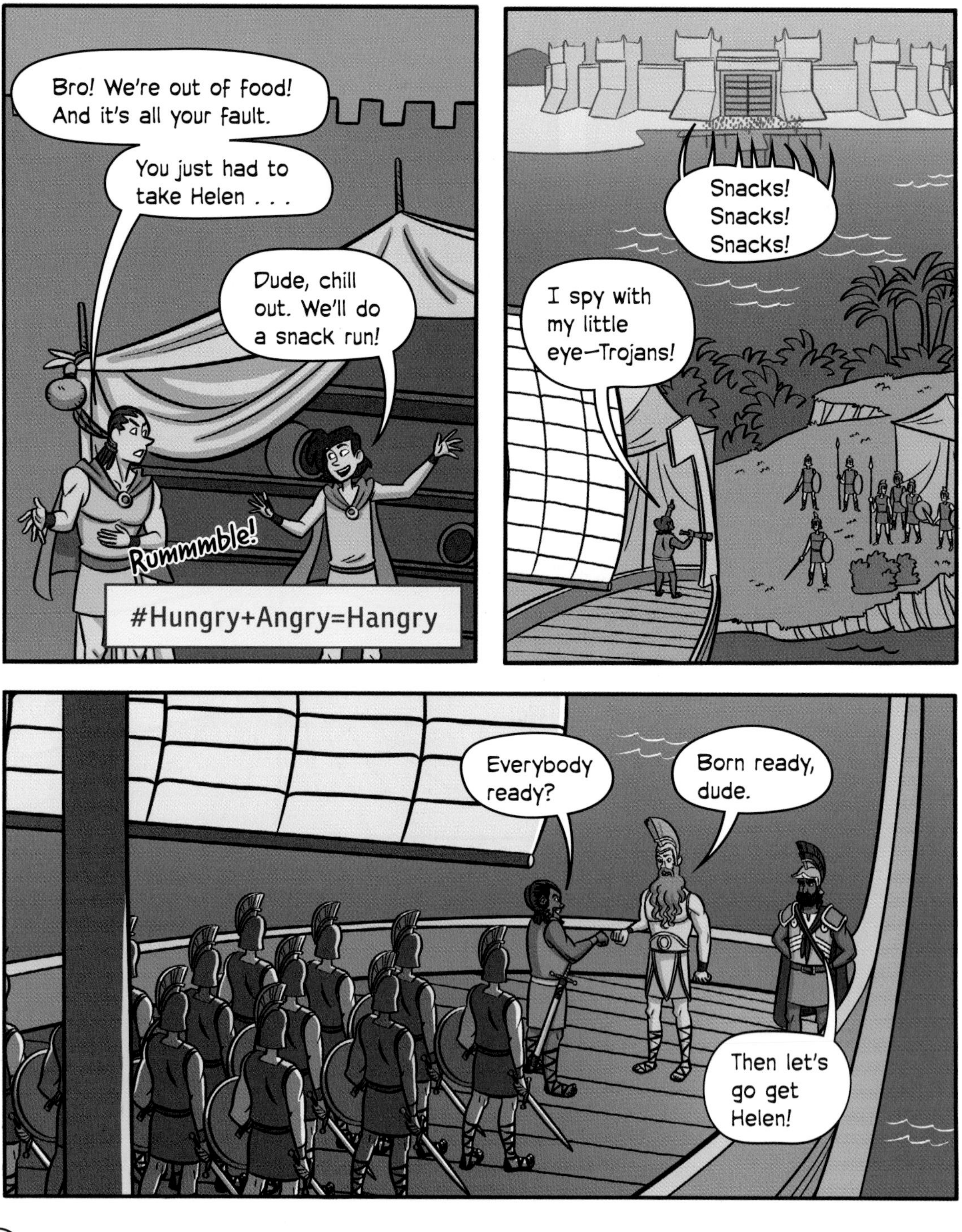
Bro! We're out of food! And it's all your fault.
You just had to take Helen . . .
Dude, chill out. We'll do a snack run!
Rummmble!
#Hungry+Angry=Hangry
Snacks! Snacks! Snacks!
I spy with my little eye—Trojans!
Everybody ready?
Born ready, dude.
Then let's go get Helen!

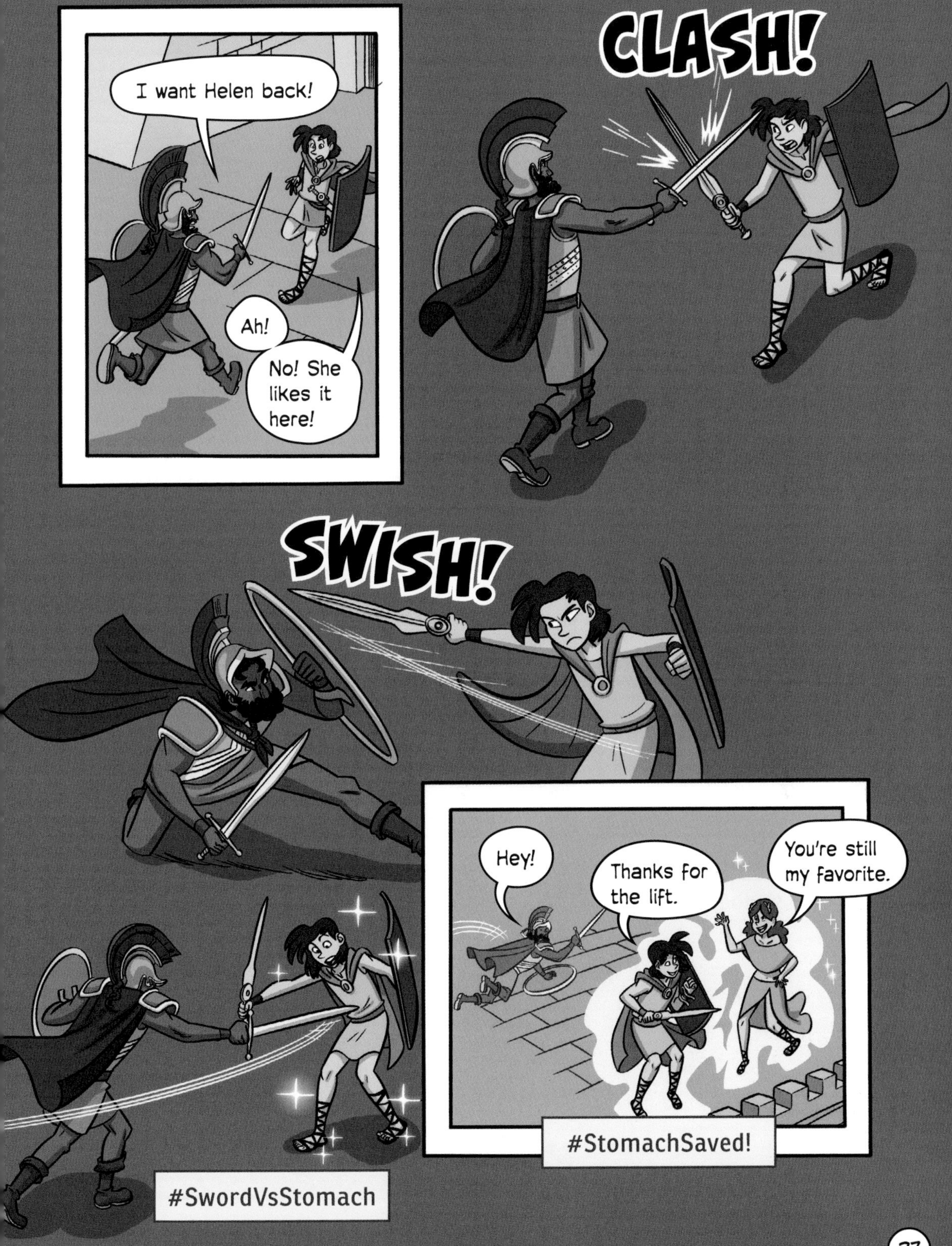
I want Helen back!
Ah!
No! She likes it here!
CLASH!
SWISH!
#SwordVsStomach
Hey!
Thanks for the lift.
You're still my favorite.
#StomachSaved!

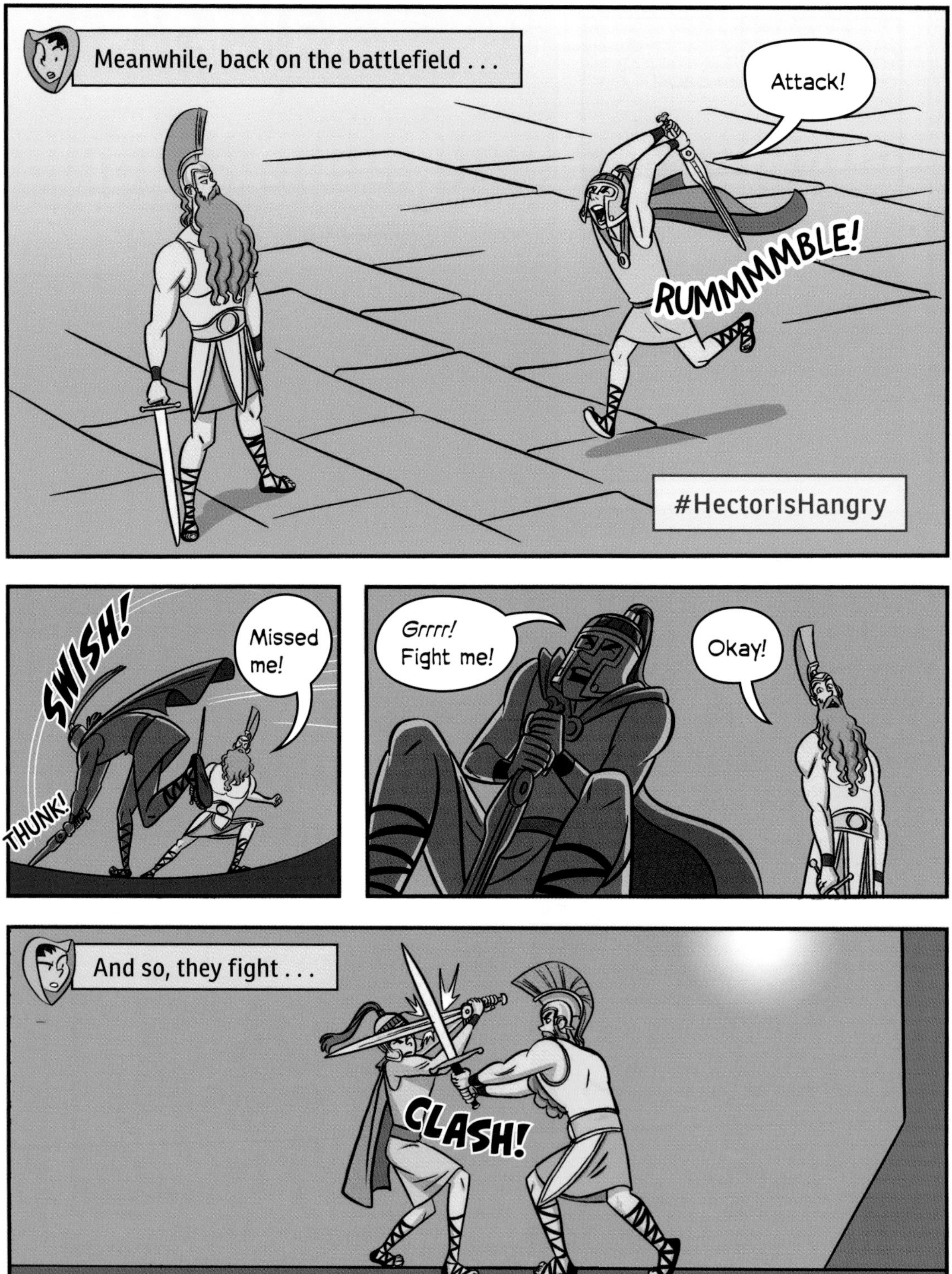
Meanwhile, back on the battlefield . . .
Attack!
RUMMMMBLE!
#HectorIsHangry
SWISH!
THUNK!
Missed me!
Grrrr! Fight me!
Okay!
And so, they fight . . .
CLASH!

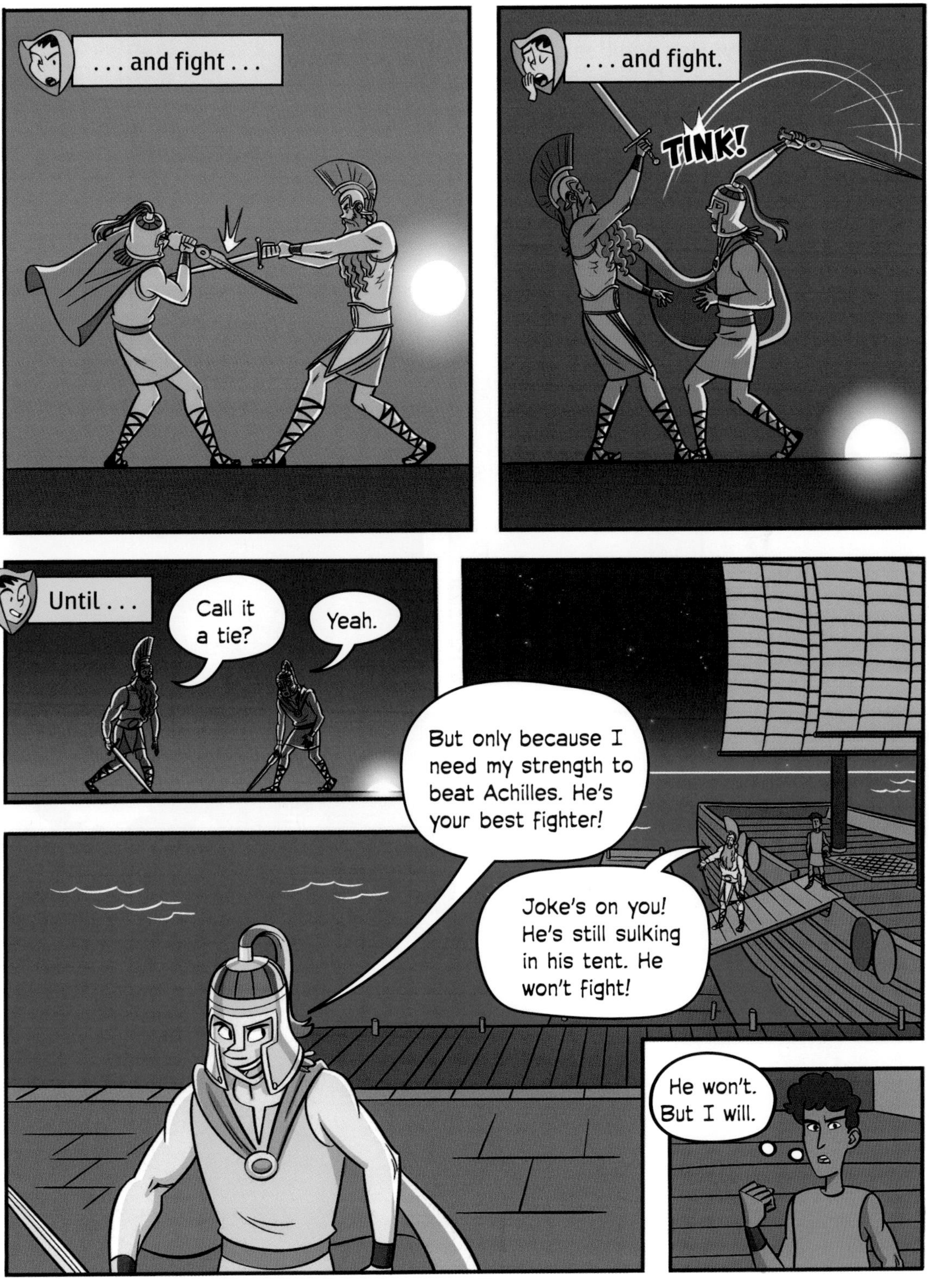
. . . and fight . . .
. . . and fight.
TINK!
Until . . .
Call it a tie?
Yeah.
But only because I need my strength to beat Achilles. He's your best fighter!
Joke's on you! He's still sulking in his tent. He won't fight!
He won't. But I will.

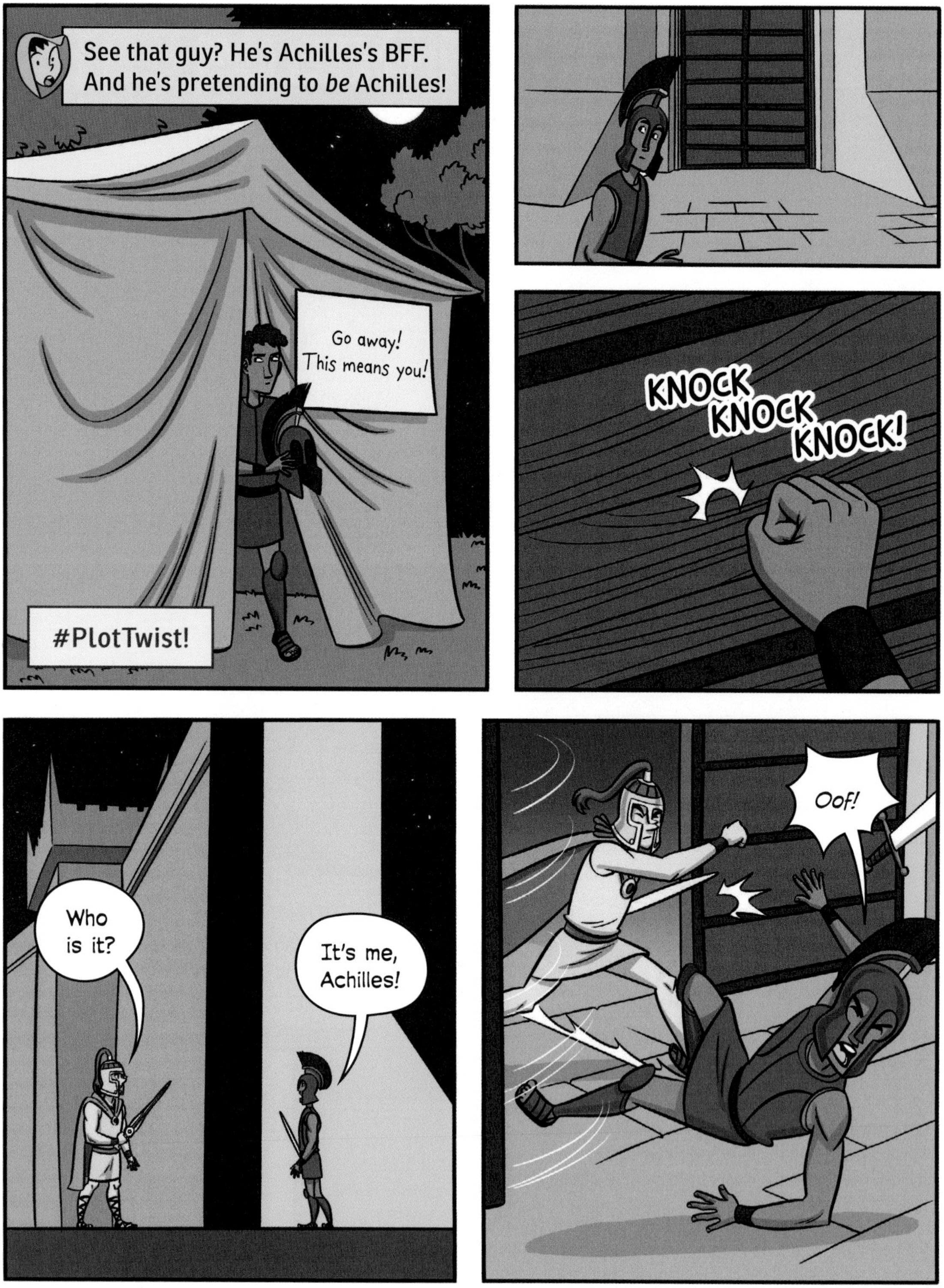
See that guy? He's Achilles's BFF. And he's pretending to *be* Achilles!
Go away! This means you!
#PlotTwist!
KNOCK KNOCK KNOCK!
Who is it?
It's me, Achilles!
Oof!

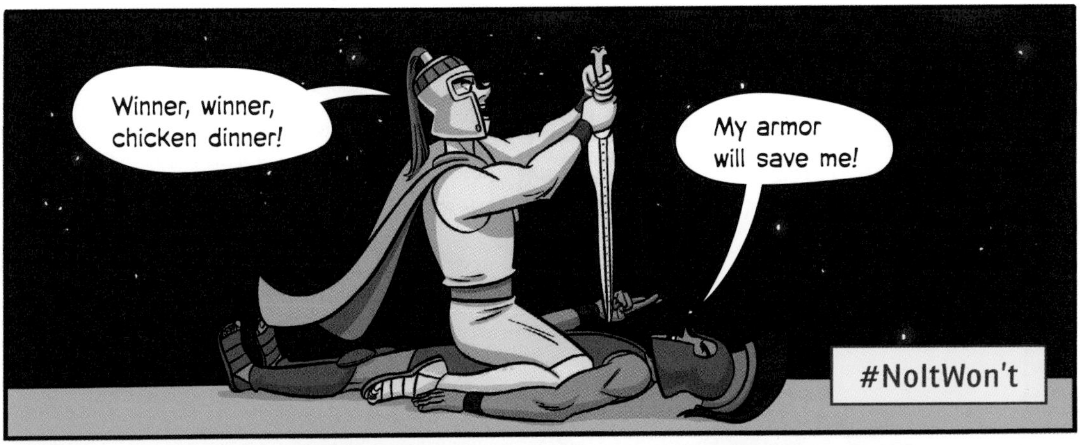
Winner, winner, chicken dinner!
My armor will save me!
#NoItWon't

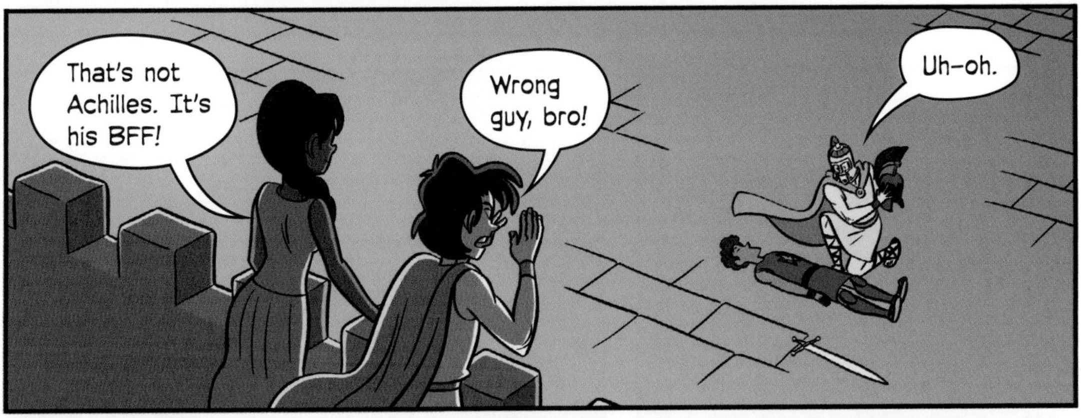
That's not Achilles. It's his BFF!
Wrong guy, bro!
Uh-oh.

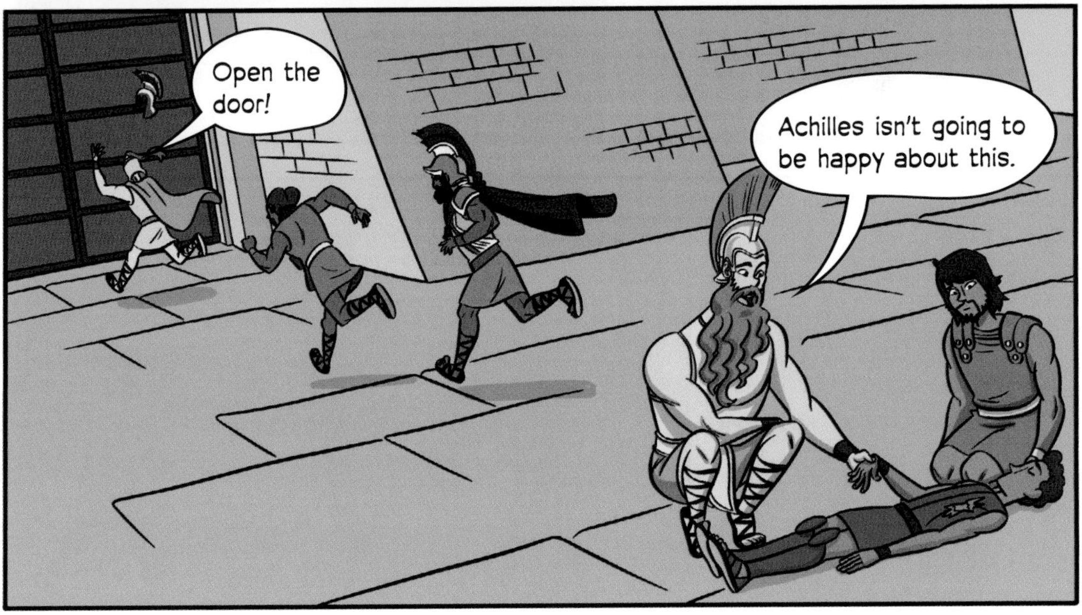
Open the door!
Achilles isn't going to be happy about this.

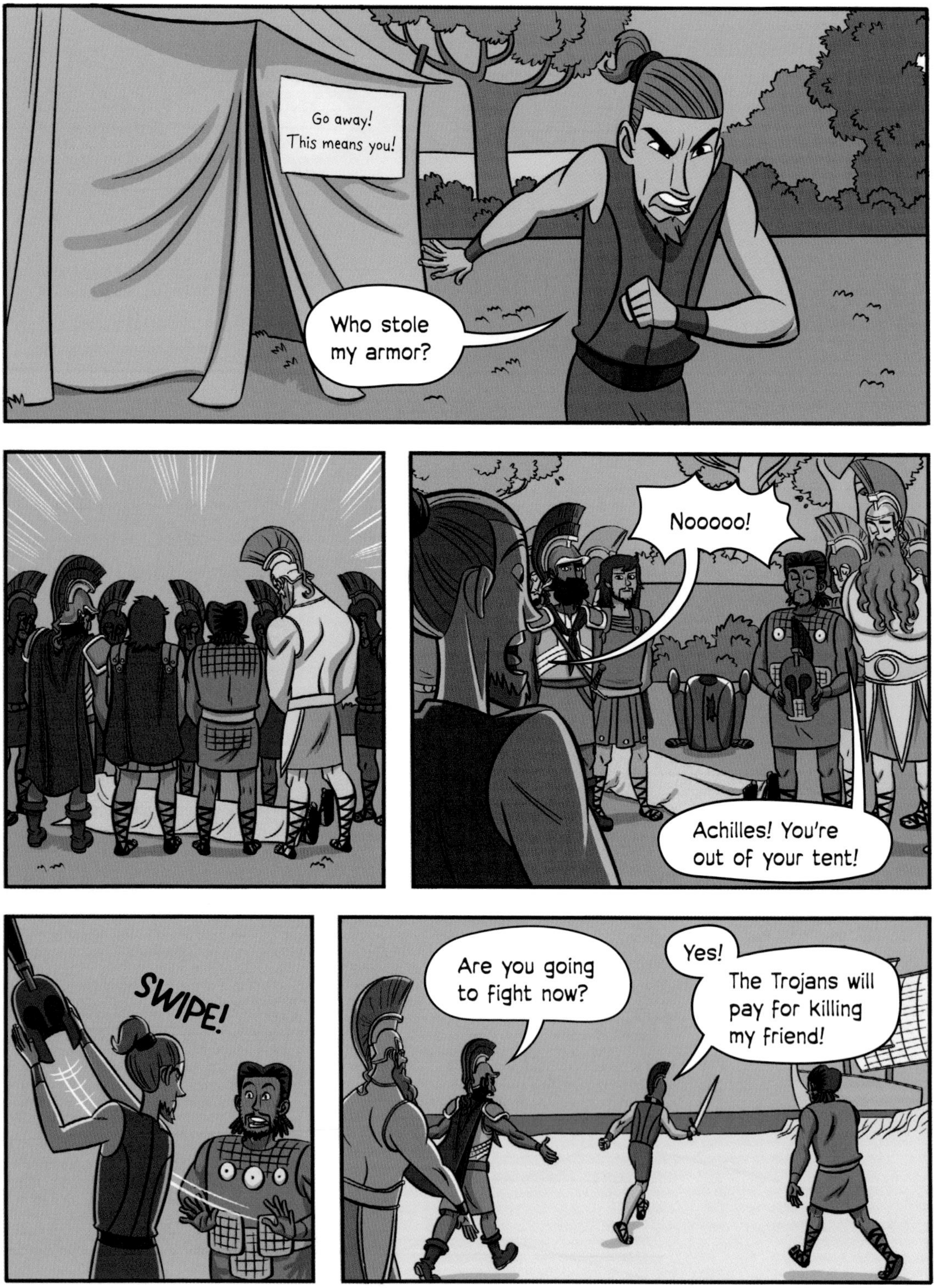
Go away!
This means you!
Who stole my armor?
Nooooo!
Achilles! You're out of your tent!
SWIPE!
Are you going to fight now?
Yes!
The Trojans will pay for killing my friend!

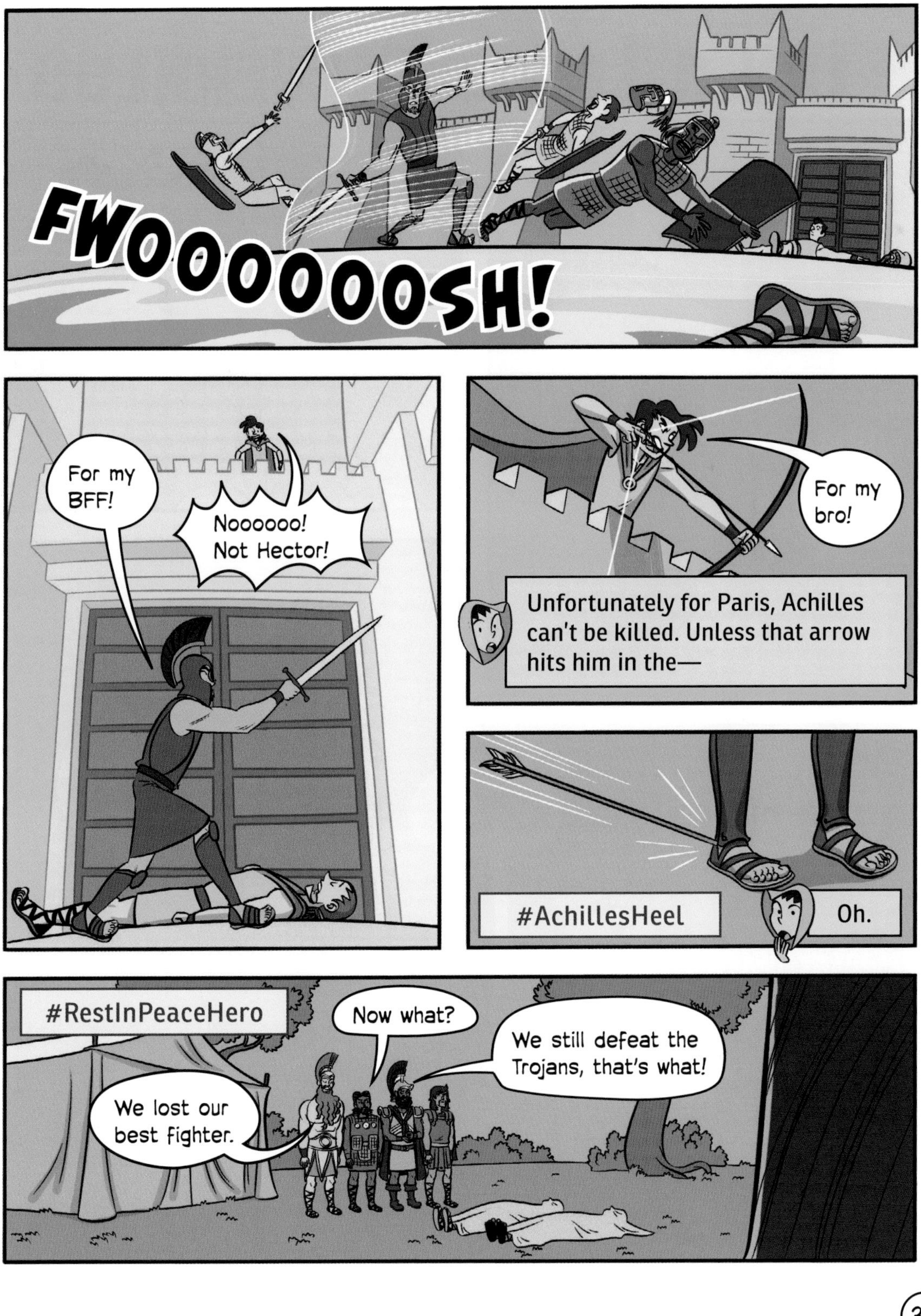

FWOOOOOOSH!
For my BFF!
Noooooo! Not Hector!
For my bro!
Unfortunately for Paris, Achilles can't be killed. Unless that arrow hits him in the—
#AchillesHeel
Oh.
#RestInPeaceHero
We lost our best fighter.
Now what?
We still defeat the Trojans, that's what!

CHAPTER 5

TRY A LITTLE CLEVERNESS

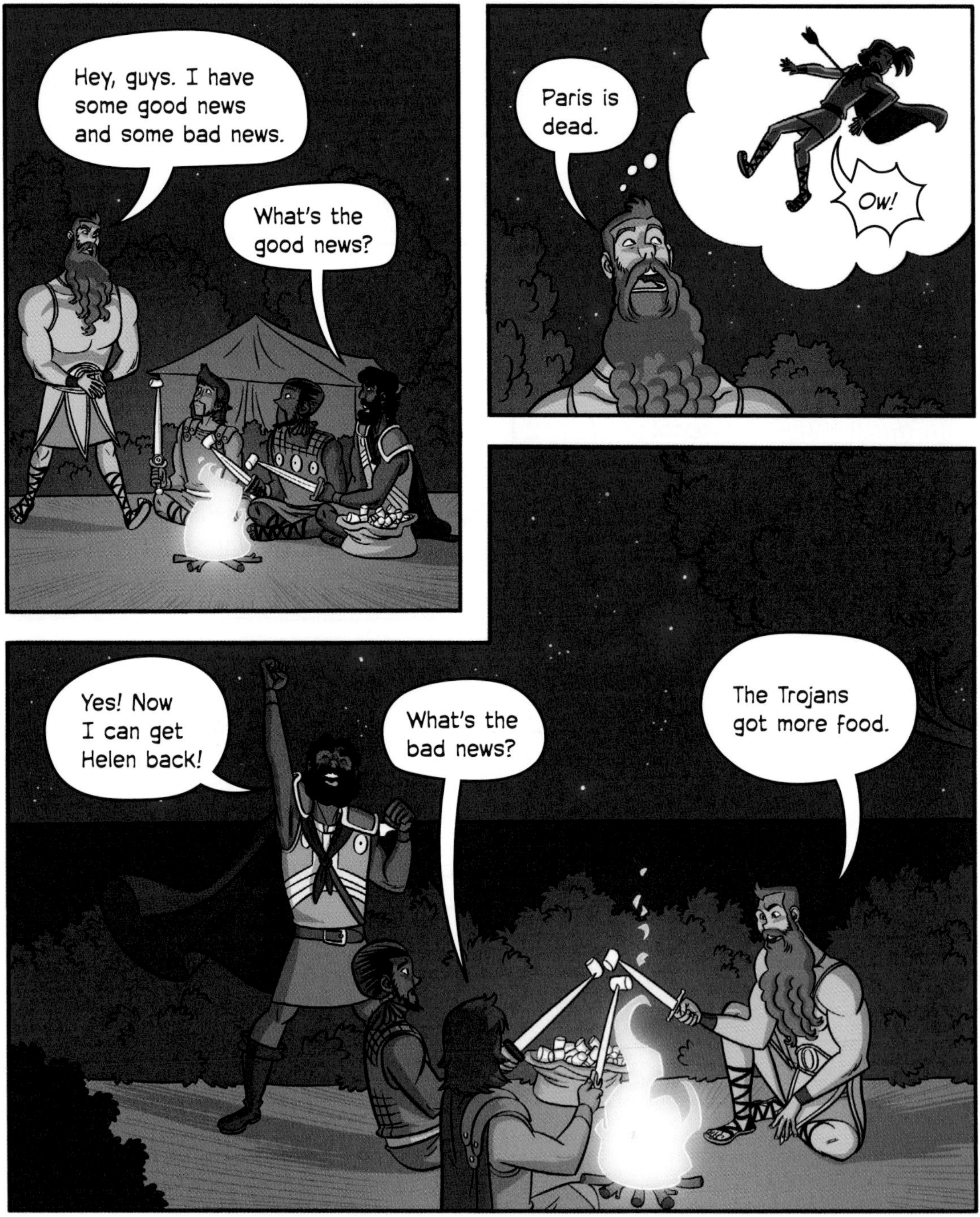

Hey, guys. I have some good news and some bad news.
What's the good news?
Paris is dead.
Ow!
Yes! Now I can get Helen back!
What's the bad news?
The Trojans got more food.

Okay, so they're not coming out. Maybe we can get in!

How?

With this! It's just a little something I've been working on in between battles.

A wooden horse?

I don't get it.

We hide inside. Then we trick the Trojans into bringing the horse into the city.

And once we're in—

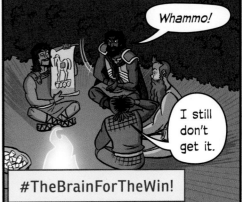

Whammo!

I still don't get it.

#TheBrainForTheWin!

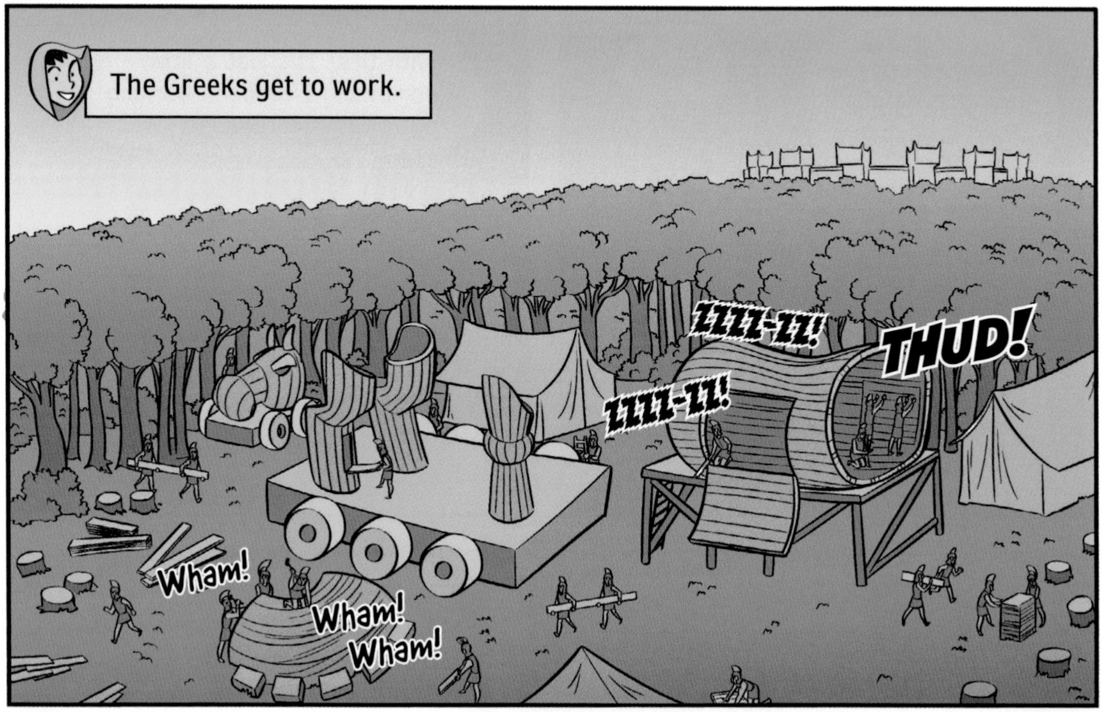
The Greeks get to work.
ZZZZ-ZZ!
THUD!
ZZZZ-ZZ!
Wham!
Wham!
Wham!

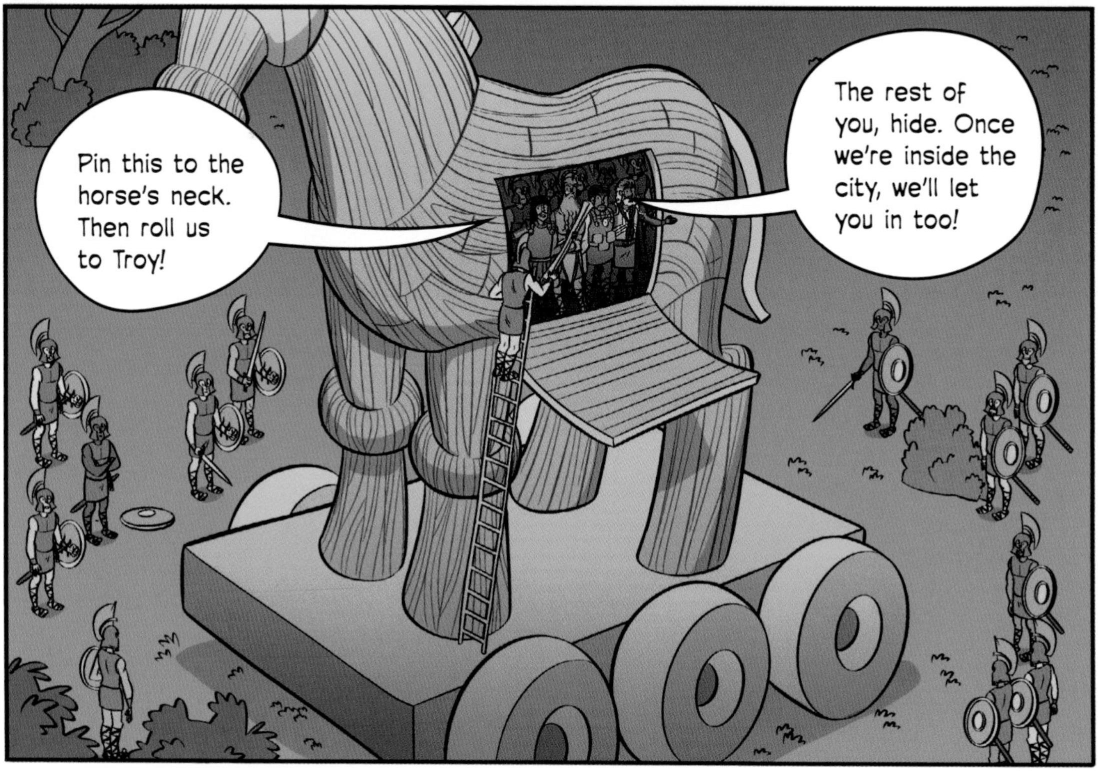
Pin this to the horse's neck. Then roll us to Troy!
The rest of you, hide. Once we're inside the city, we'll let you in too!

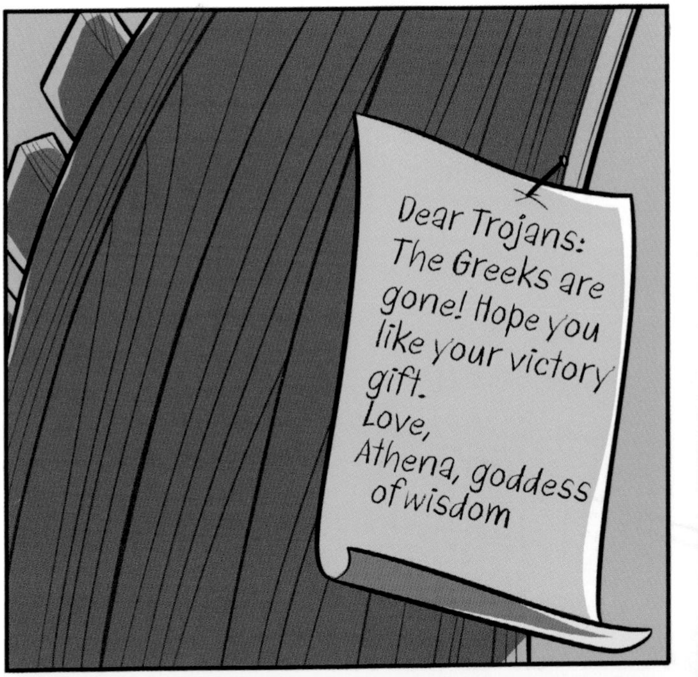
Dear Trojans:
The Greeks are gone! Hope you like your victory gift.
Love,
Athena, goddess of wisdom

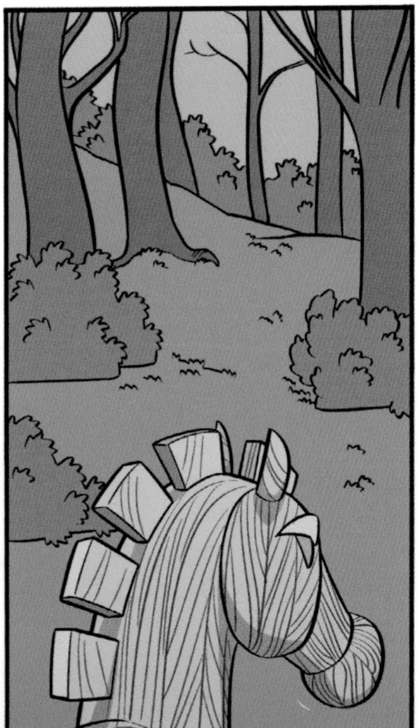

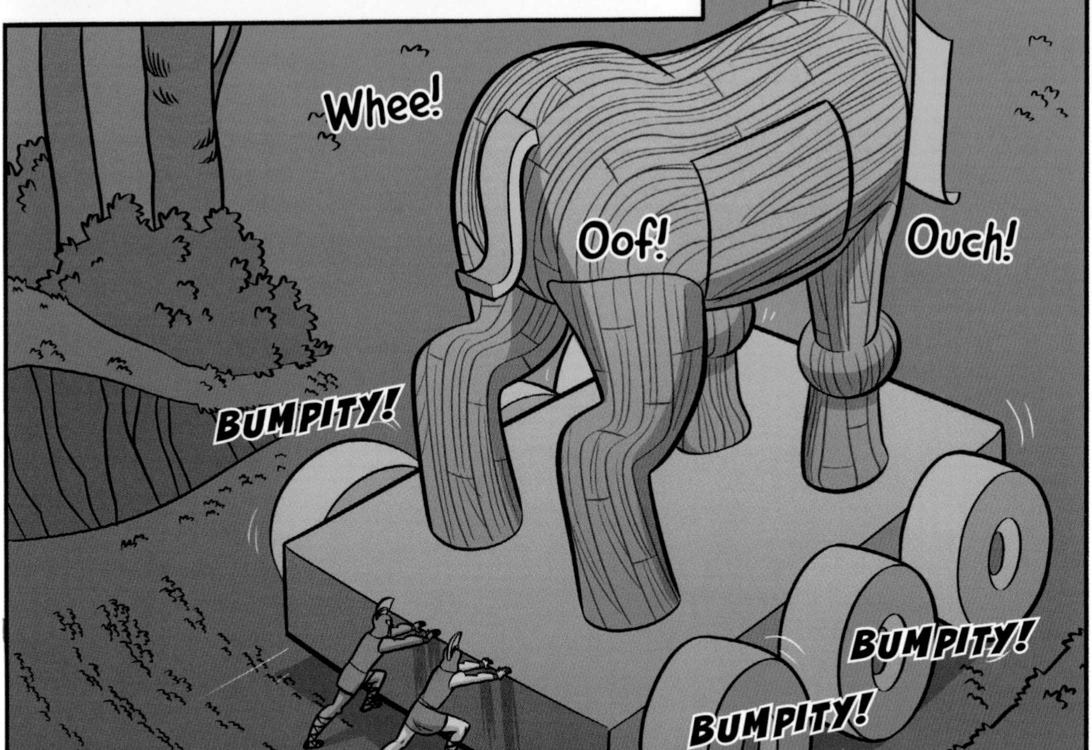
Whee!
Oof!
Ouch!
BUMPITY!
BUMPITY!
BUMPITY!

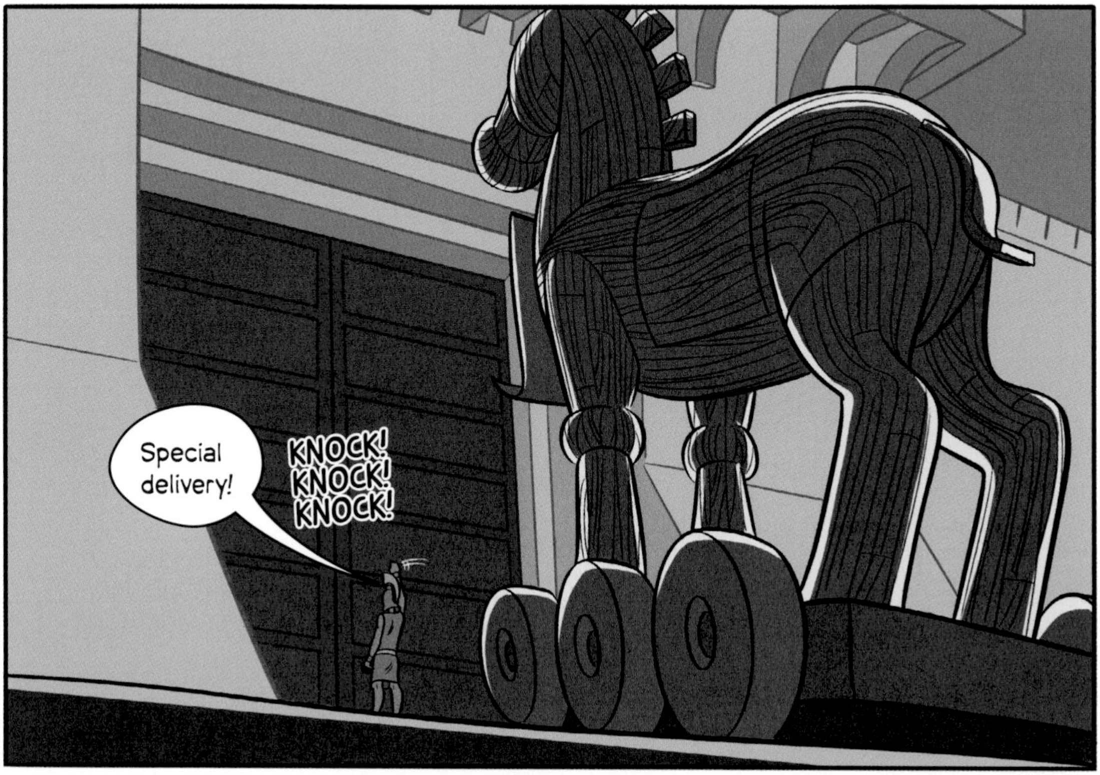
Special delivery!
KNOCK! KNOCK! KNOCK!

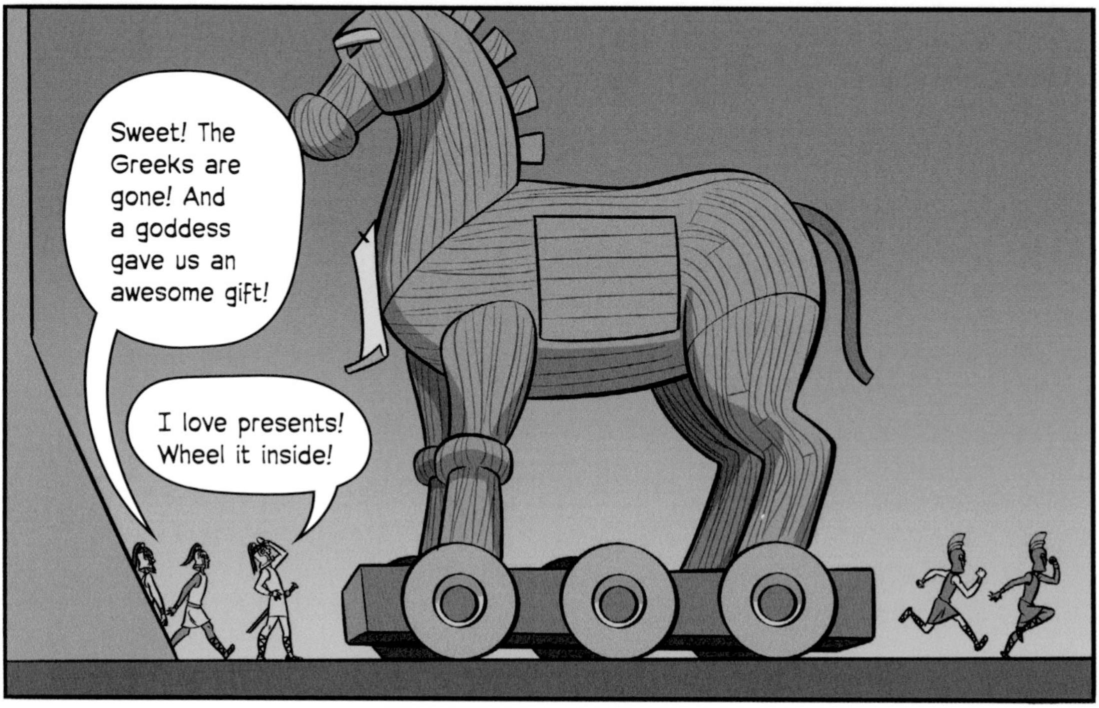
Sweet! The Greeks are gone! And a goddess gave us an awesome gift!
I love presents! Wheel it inside!

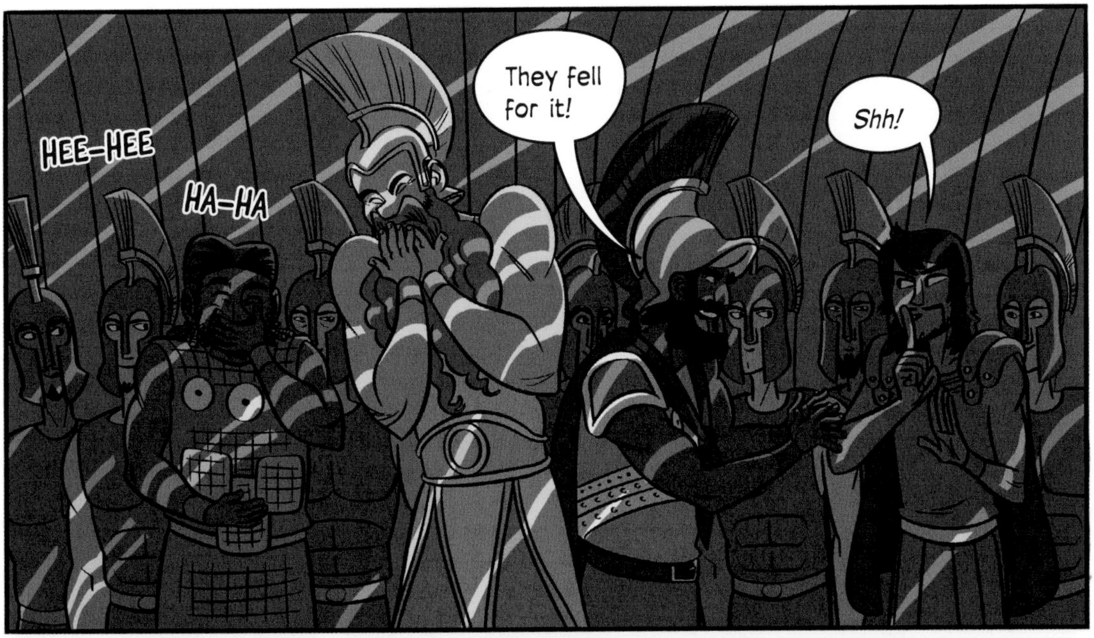
HEE-HEE
HA-HA
They fell for it!
Shh!

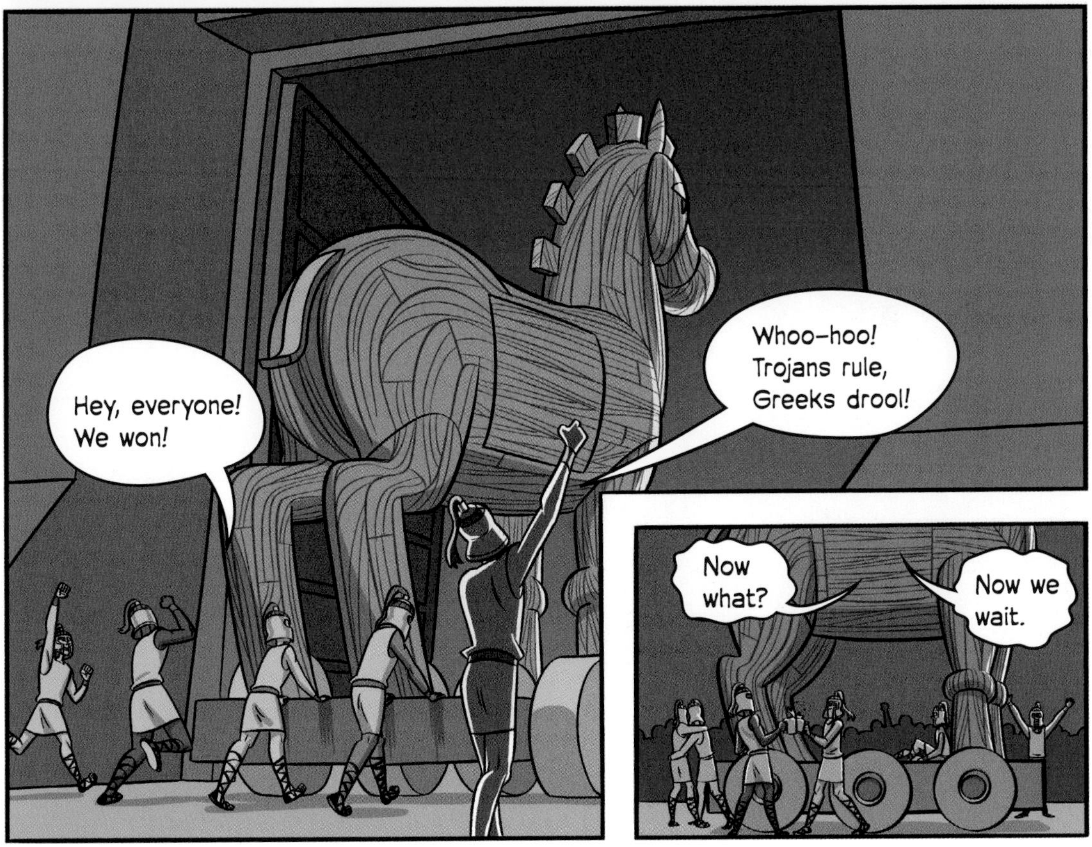
Hey, everyone! We won!
Whoo-hoo! Trojans rule, Greeks drool!
Now what?
Now we wait.

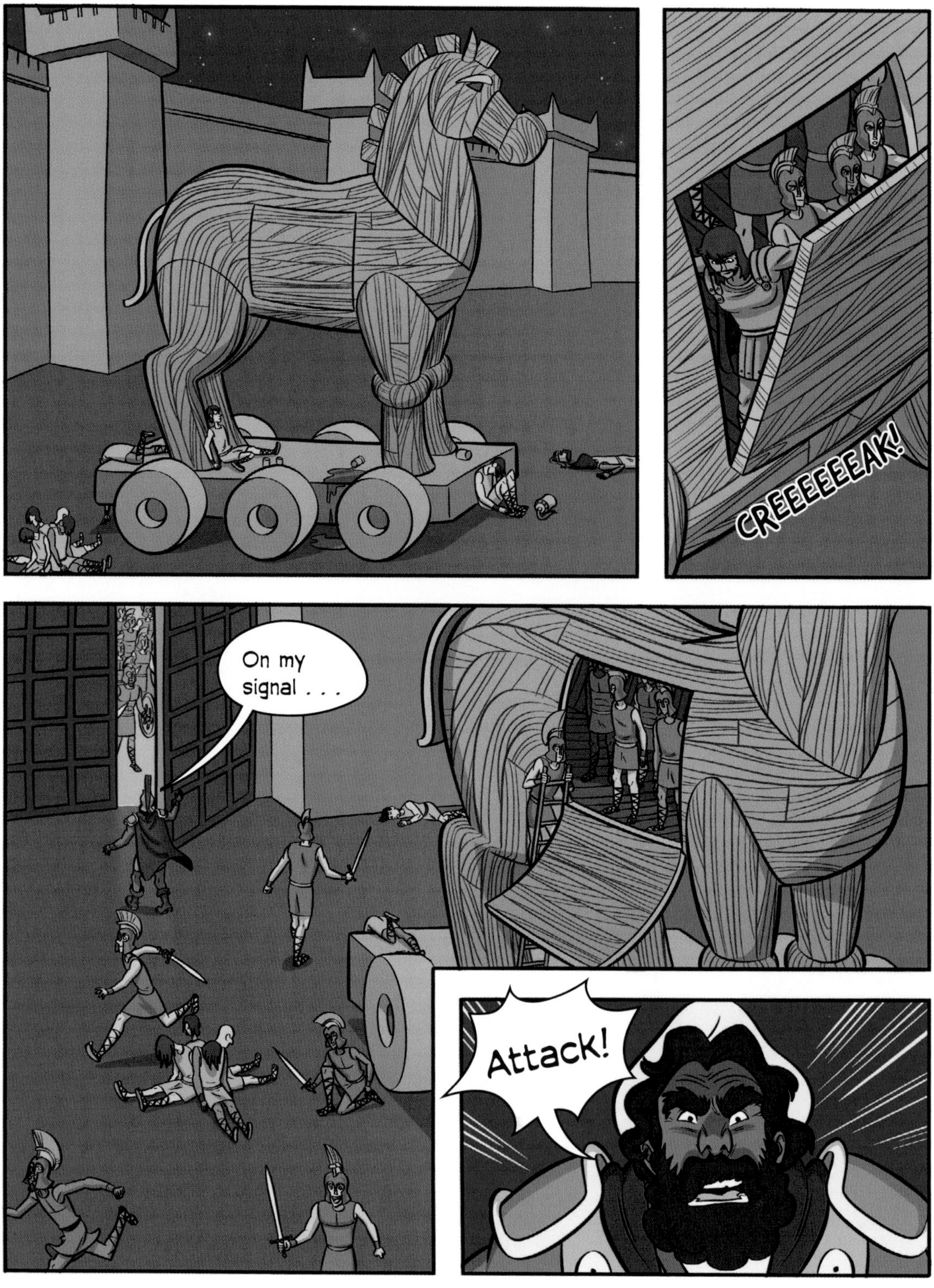
CREEEEEEAK!
On my signal . . .
Attack!

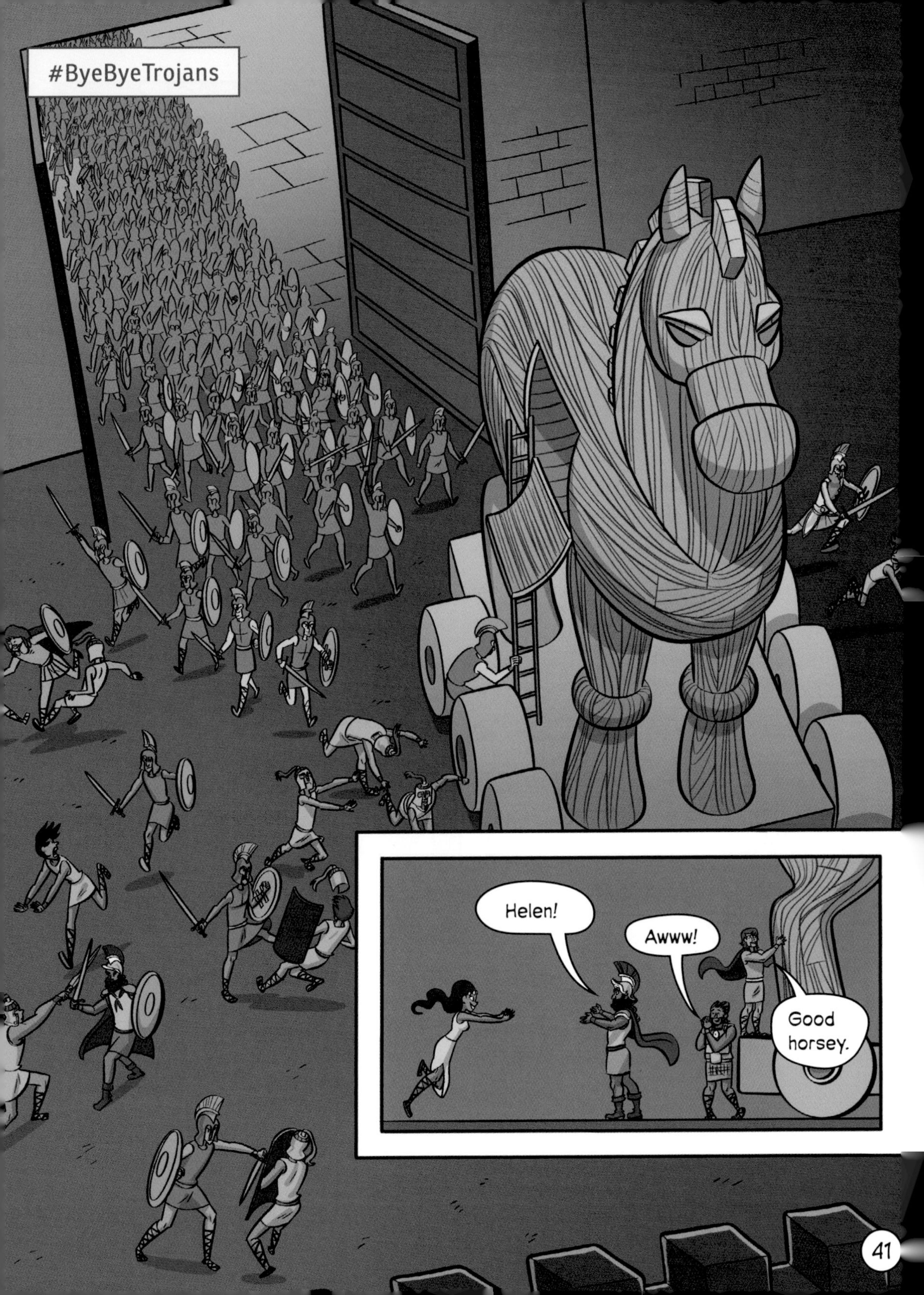
#ByeByeTrojans
Helen!
Awww!
Good horsey.

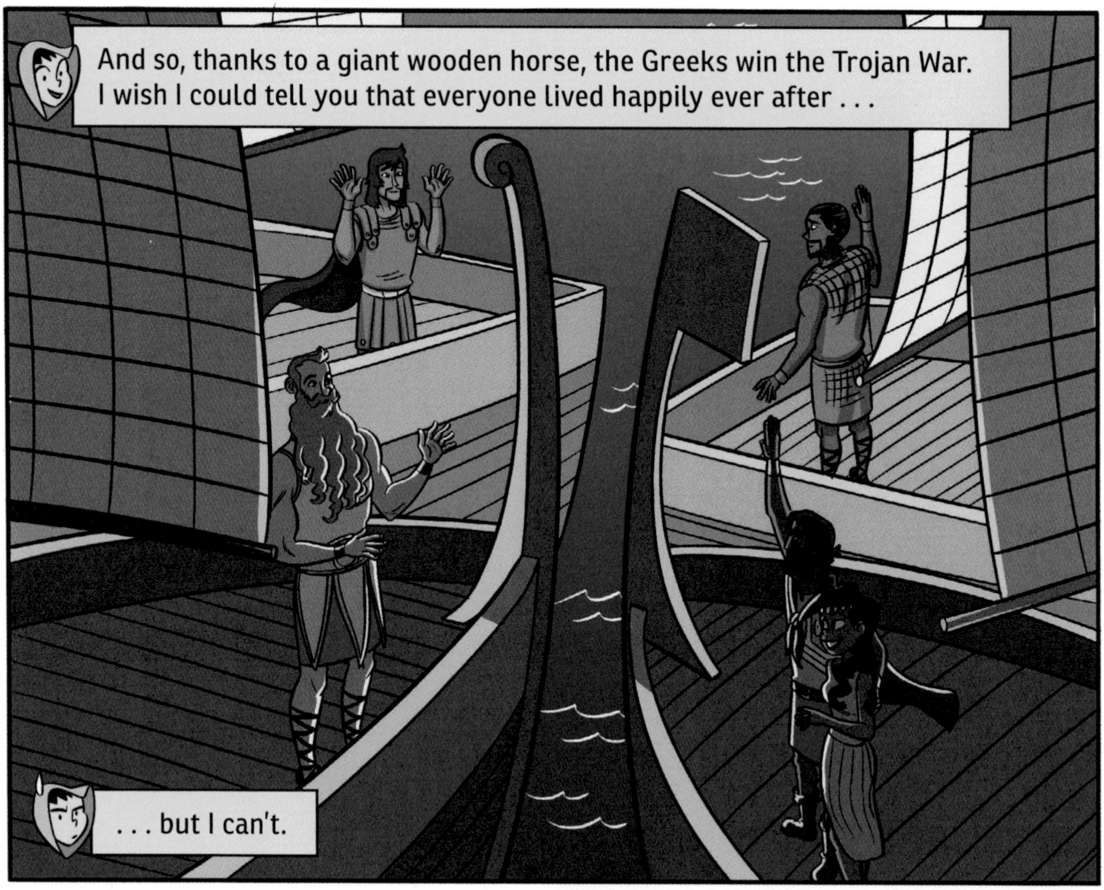
And so, thanks to a giant wooden horse, the Greeks win the Trojan War. I wish I could tell you that everyone lived happily ever after . . .
. . . but I can't.
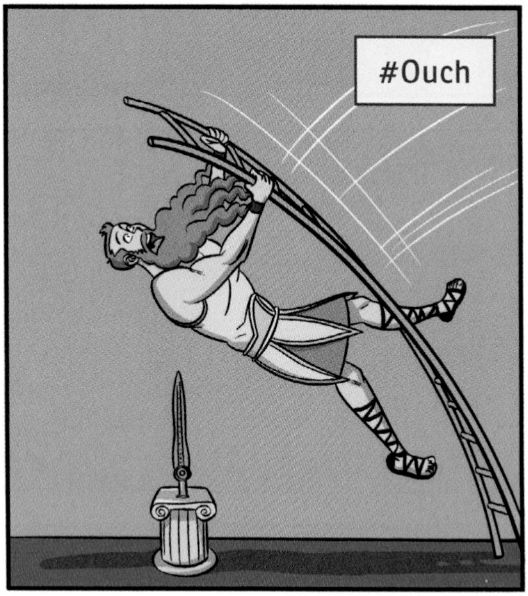
#Ouch
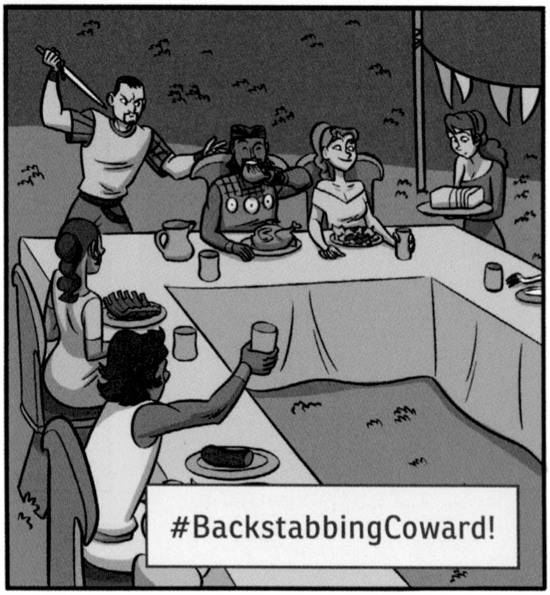
#BackstabbingCoward!

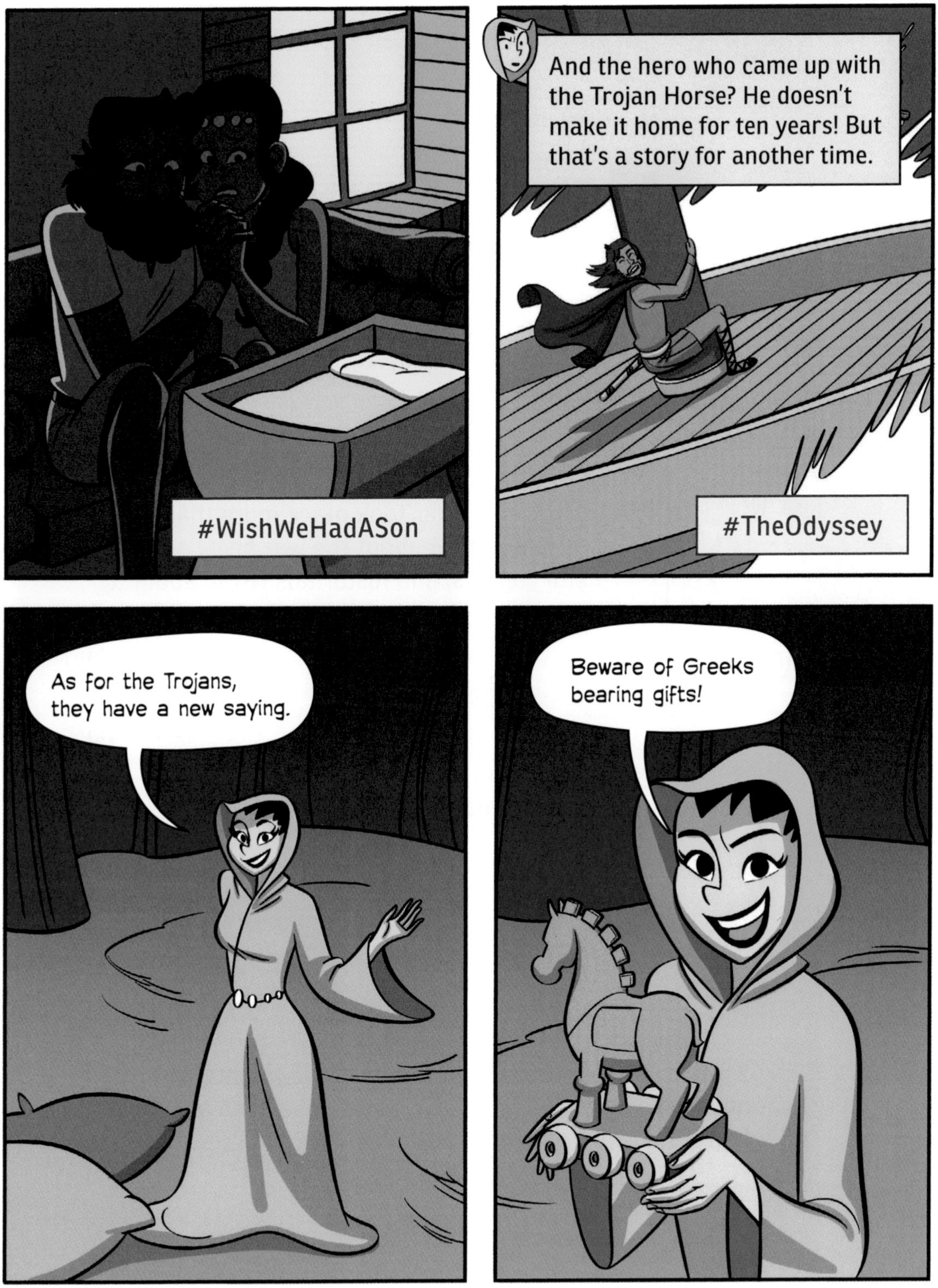
#WishWeHadASon
And the hero who came up with the Trojan Horse? He doesn't make it home for ten years! But that's a story for another time.
#TheOdyssey
As for the Trojans, they have a new saying.
Beware of Greeks bearing gifts!

MORE ABOUT THE TROJAN HORSE

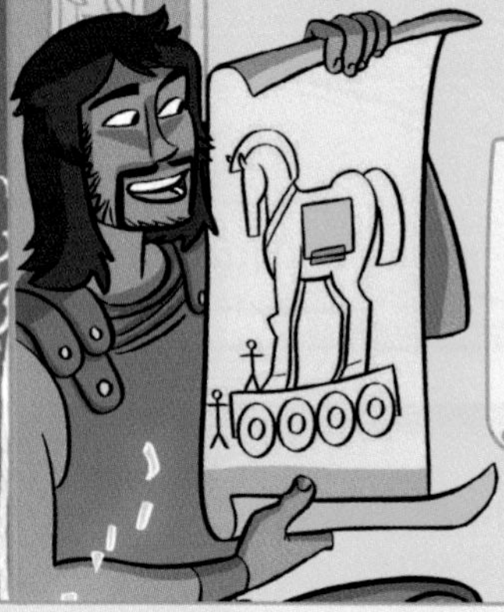

The Trojan War took place more than 3,000 years ago. We know about the war because ancient poets, storytellers, and historians wrote about it.

According to the myth, the Greeks built the giant wooden horse in three days.

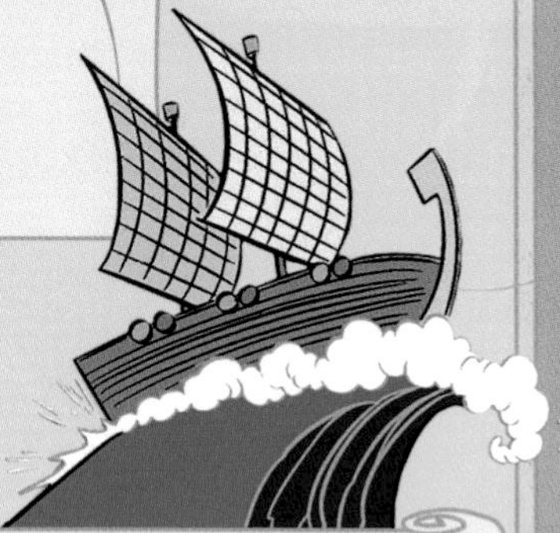

Some historians think the wooden horse might not have been a horse after all. It might have been a battering ram or a ship that looked like a horse.

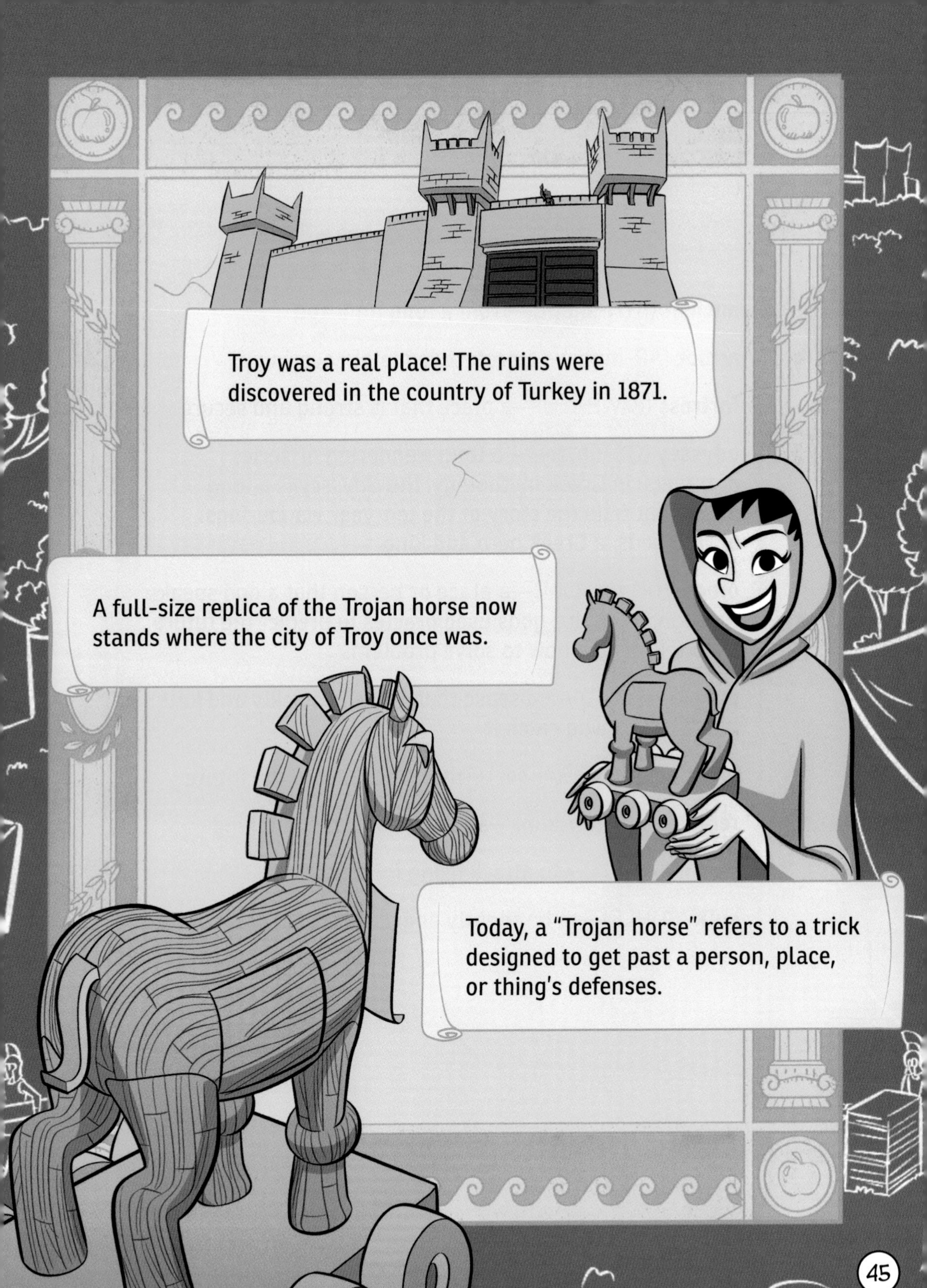

Troy was a real place! The ruins were discovered in the country of Turkey in 1871.
A full-size replica of the Trojan horse now stands where the city of Troy once was.
Today, a "Trojan horse" refers to a trick designed to get past a person, place, or thing's defenses.

Glossary

ancient (AYN-shunt)—from a long time ago

armor (AR-muhr)—a protective metal covering

fortress (FAWR-tris)—a place that is strong and secure

odyssey (OD-uh-see)—a long wandering or series of travels; in Greek mythology, the *Odyssey* is a long poem that tells the story of the ten-year wanderings of Odysseus, a Greek hero and king

oracle (OR-uh-kuhl)—a place or person that a god speaks through; in myths, gods used oracles to predict the future or to tell people how to solve problems

plague (PLAYG)—a disease that spreads quickly and kills most people who catch it

prophecy (PROF-uh-see)—the foretelling of the future

replica (REP-luh-kuh)—an exact copy of something

storm (STORM)—to attack using force

sulk (SUHLK)—to be silently angry, upset, or irritable

INTERNET SITES

DK Find Out!: The Trojan Horse
dkfindout.com/us/history/ancient-greece/trojan-horse/

History for Kids: Trojan Horse
historyforkids.net/trojan-horse.html

Kiddle: Trojan War facts for kids
kids.kiddle.co/Trojan_War

OTHER BOOKS IN THIS SERIES

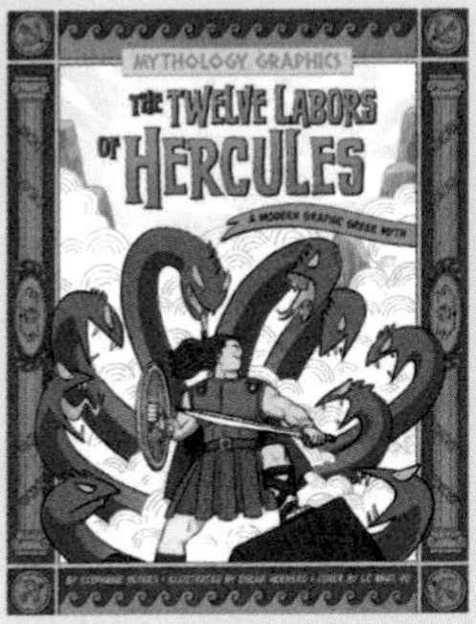
MYTHOLOGY GRAPHICS
THE TWELVE LABORS OF HERCULES

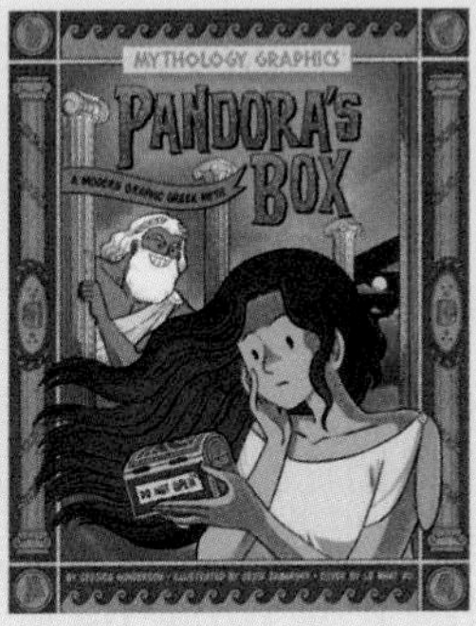
MYTHOLOGY GRAPHICS
PANDORA'S BOX

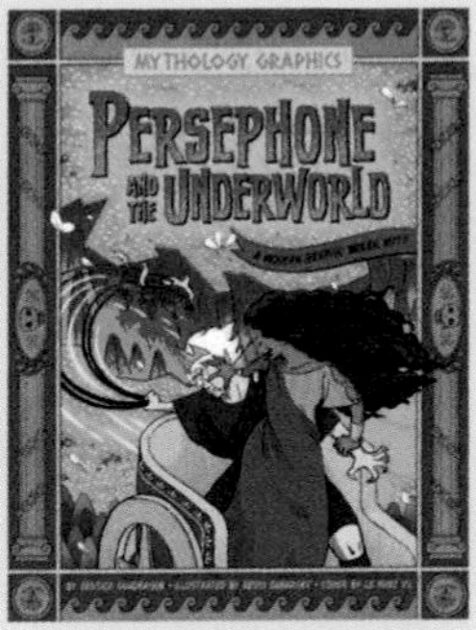
MYTHOLOGY GRAPHICS
PERSEPHONE AND THE UNDERWORLD

About the Creators

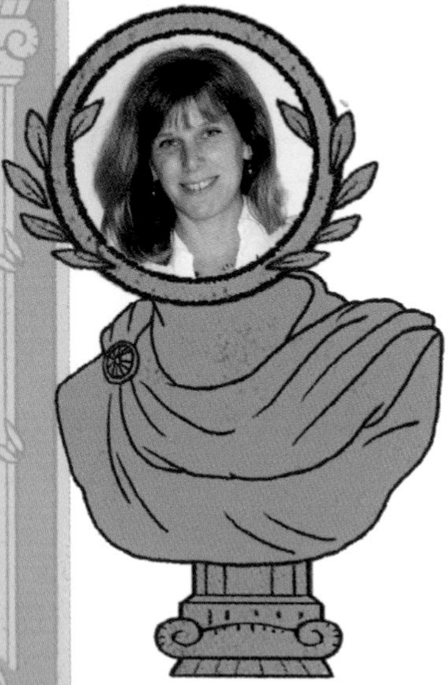

Stephanie Peters has been writing books for children for more than twenty-five years. Her most recent Capstone titles include *Earth's Amazing Journey: From Pebbles to Continents* and *The Twelve Labors of Hercules: A Modern Graphic Greek Myth* from the Mythology Graphics series. An avid reader, workout enthusiast, and beach wanderer, Stephanie enjoys spending time with her family and their pets. She lives and works in Mansfield, Massachusetts.
Photo Credit: Daniel Peters

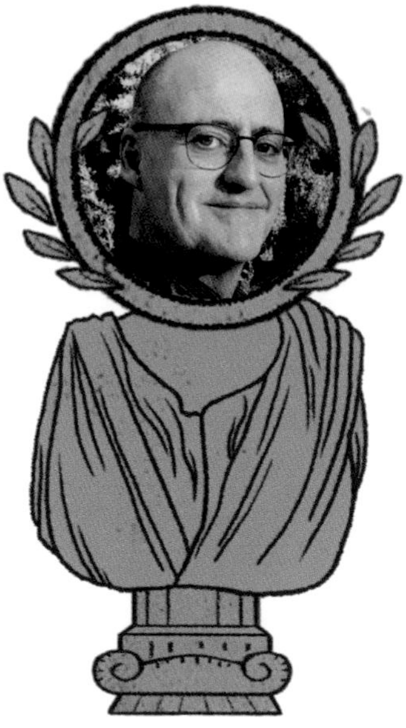

Oscar Herrero was born in Madrid, Spain, and studied journalism before deciding to devote himself entirely to art. He is an illustrator, character designer, and writer with experience illustrating children's books, comics, magazine covers, album cover art, and video games, as well as working as a visual development artist for leading animation studios.
Photo Credit: Diana Herrero

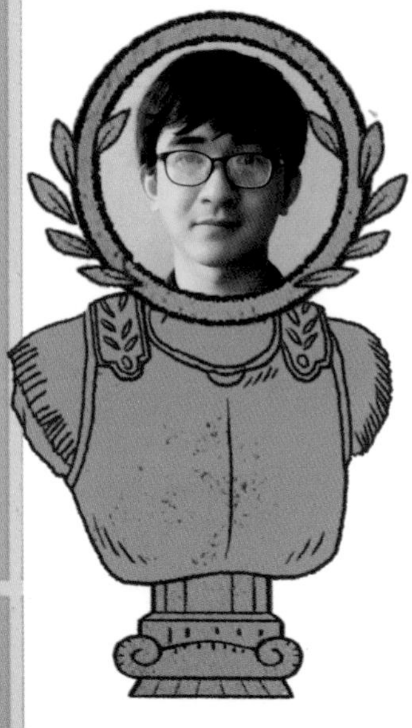

Le Nhat Vu was born in Nha Trang, a seaside city in Vietnam. He now works as a book illustrator in Ho Chi Minh City. He draws inspiration from fantasy, adventure, and poetic stories. During his free time, he enjoys reading Japanese comics (manga) or novels, watching football or movies—maybe with a cup of milk coffee.
Photo Credit: Le Nhat Vu